What's It All About, Sybil?

What's It All About, Sybil?

The Sybil Jason International Fan Club:26 Years of Excerpts From Newsletters That I Wrote To My Fan Club Members

Sybil Jason

BearManor Media

2010

What's It All About, Sybil?
The Sybil Jason International Fan Club:
26 Years of Excerpts From Newsletters
That I Wrote To My Fan Club Members

© 2010 Sybil Jason

For information, address:

BearManor Media
P. O. Box 71426
Albany, GA 31708

bearmanormedia.com

Cover design by John Teehan

Typesetting and layout by John Teehan

Published in the USA by BearManor Media

ISBN—1-59393-540-4

Table of Contents

Foreword

This part of my book is essentially the same as *My Fifteen Minutes* and *Five Minutes More* because it entails memories of the past. However, it also interlocks those past eras with some of my most recent 26 years of show-business activities. Please note that I said my show business *activities* rather than my show-business *career*. There *is* a difference, but exciting just the same.

To the best of my knowledge and memory, this all started around the mid-1970s when the public seemed to be in a very nostalgic mood and fell in love, once again, with the Hollywood of the '30s and '40s. Sensing that this renewed interest would grow, a lot of organizations started to form with the intent of honoring the Golden Era of Hollywood and its stars. Fortunately, many of these icons were still alive and had retained that certain magic that had made them famous in the first place. However, it was no easy job finding these stars because many of them had involuntarily retired due to the advent on the Hollywood scene of a group of very bright, upcoming directors, producers and writers who were taking giant steps into the new future of Hollywood. For the most part, this did not include using the stars from the past two eras. It was not a matter of blackballing anyone because if an icon of the past fit into a scenario that needed a mature character, the young executives used them and were appreciative that these professionals undoubtedly enhanced the quality of their productions. But the true name of the game was "That was *then* and this is *now!*" and it took a lot of courage for these former stars to make the adjustment to becoming featured players. Some of them saw the writing on the wall before things started to change and decided to retire from acting before being reduced in status. Most of my contemporaries were still young enough to want to go on with their careers. However, after I heard some of the horror stories they told while trying to get a grip hold on their careers as young adults, I decided that that was one direction I just didn't want to approach. As it was, I was happily married and had a beautiful baby daughter and had a busy and active life. In my past two books you read how very active it was, so it would be redundant to repeat it all over again. But I will say that as these organizations became more and more popular, my husband and I attended a minimum of two to three banquets a month and I won't skirt the fact that it was wonderful for the ego. For most of us, treading the "down-to-earth" cement had become a daily occurrence for quite a while, but, now, all of a sudden, out rolled the red carpet for us to tread on once again.

There also entered an additional new phase in my life which was completely unexpected and continues on to this very day.

In 1983, there was a theatre on Wilshire Boulevard in Los Angeles called The Vagabond, which ran popular movies of the '30s and '40s. One week they were featuring a double bill of *The Little Princess* and *The Blue Bird*, and they asked me to please attend as a special guest.

The theatre was packed with an appreciative audience and at intermission time many people approached me to question me about the parts that I played in both movies and the inevitable questions of how I liked working with Shirley Temple and if we got along. There was one particular gentleman who seemed extremely interested in my own career at Warner Bros. and was quite knowledgeable that before I came to Fox and worked alongside of Shirley, I had starred in my own movies at Warners and he remembered quite a few of them. Before it was time to return to our seats, he mentioned that he was just on a visit to California from Nebraska, but he hoped that on his next trip to California he would be able to meet me once again. That was not too long in the coming.

Although my husband, Tony, and I attended many banquets honoring those of us from the Golden Era, we did have our favorite organizations and attended them yearly. One of them was The Jeanette MacDonald Fan Club and it was always fun being on the dais with so many interesting guest stars, some of whom I had never met before.

At the end of this particular MacDonald banquet, the gentleman from Nebraska came up to me and reminded me that we had met at The Vagabond a number of months previously. I am ashamed to say that I am very bad at remembering names, but I *never* forget a face even if many years have gone by. In this case, it was only a matter of a few months and

I told him that I remembered him very well. We talked briefly about what a nice banquet it had been and how interesting the guests were and what they had to say up on the mike. After a while, he changed the subject and, to my amazement, said that he wanted to start a fan club for me and asked if I would approve of it.

Well, to be very honest and certainly not to be rude to this nice gentleman, it was all I could do to stifle a giggle at this suggestion. I couldn't imagine who would join such a club as it had been years since I had been in the public eye. In a gentle way I explained that I was very flattered by his suggestion, but I could only imagine what an uphill battle it would be for him to get members and, as much as I loved the idea, I didn't think it would work out. After I thanked Gary L. Heckman of Lincoln, Nebraska, very much, I declined this honor. But, still, he insisted that there were a lot of people that still remembered me from my movies and if I was willing to give him permission to start the club, he would be more than happy to do so. Very reluctantly, I gave him permission, but commented that if we lasted a year I would be very surprised, but extremely flattered nonetheless.

In a matter of two years' time, our club became International and, much to my awe but to Gary's "I told you so" grin, we are now in our twenty-sixth year of the fan club.

This following newsletter to the members of my fan club is an explanation of the steps, mishaps, disappointments, but ultimate the joy of trying to and finally finding a publisher for my first book and autobiography, *My Fifteen Minutes*.

In this wondrous age of electronics, I found that inhabiting the world of the computer was to be a mixed blessing made up of a potpourri of frustration, but also of wild accomplishment! My first book was written on a typewriter and that method, although quite archaic in 2005, felt comfortable to me, but admittedly proved to be a lot of work before I could safely say that I had a decent final copy to send to a prospective publisher. That acceptable copy proved to be a "walk in the park" in comparison to my trying to find a publisher for it! Through the hit and miss that a lot of neophyte authors go through, it was not long before I learned that to send out just *one* copy of my manuscript and then to wait for a reply, which took anywhere from four to six weeks' time, was not very productive. Sometimes there were no replies at all!

As frustrating as that was, the most puzzling to me were the replies from the publishers that I *did* get. They were *very* complimentary about my style of writing and found that the contents of my book contained a lot of interesting and brand-new facts about world renown icons that had not been written before, but, ultimately, what it boiled down to was a very polite rejection. They were extremely diplomatic, but what they *really* meant to say was that the subjects of my book *and* myself were strictly *then* and they wanted *now*!

Basically, being an optimist and quite stubborn in nature, I just knew that somewhere out there there must be a publisher that would find what I had to say about the Golden Era of Hollywood interesting and there was. I found him in a delightful and unexpected way. I had been in touch with two lovely lady authors, Laura Wagner and Sandra Grabman, and, to my mind, had helped them in a minimal way with little bits of information about some of the stars that they were writing about and that I just happened to have known. Unlike me, they thought my input was very helpful and, later, just through socializing via email, I told them that, being a neophyte writer, I had just finished my autobiography and was trying to find a publisher for it.

Before I could blink an eye, these generous young lady authors *both* suggested that I must get in touch with a man named Ben Ohmart who was a publisher in love with anything to do with the Golden Era and was not afraid to take chances on stories connected with the subjects of that era. BearManor Media, at that time, was a comparatively new and small publishing company, but, thankfully for me, Ben told me to send him a copy of my book and he would take a good look at it. I can only wish that all authors had the incredible good luck to have Ben Ohmart as their publisher because, in my experience, he was everything and *more* than what Laura and Sandra said he would be.

I cannot tell you how very thrilled I was to actually see *My Fifteen Minutes* in final book form. Aside from the personal satisfaction I received, there was an even more important reason to be grateful that it was a *fait accompli* in 2005. My dear husband of 58 years, Tony Drake, had been battling a courageous fight against 4th stage lung cancer and, now, to see the light return to his beautiful blue eyes while holding the first copy of my book in his hands was a gift from Heaven. He read it every single day, over and over again, and I treasure that well-worn copy that is tucked away very carefully and lovingly in a very special place in my home.

I have been asked numerous times what made me start writing a book in the first place and I must say that it was a combination of a few things.

While lecturing on my career in theatres, colleges, women's clubs and other venues, the most prevalent question was always if I had written a book. Of course, I had never, ever considered doing it until one day I was having lunch with a friend of mine who had been in the movie industry, but not as an entertainer. We started howling with laughter about

A signed autograph picture of South African President Nelson Mandela to me. 2004

something that had happened years ago to a star I was friends with; it was an incident I had completely forgotten about until then. She said to me, after drying her tears of laughter from her eyes, "You should write a book and get stories like that down in print."

When I got home that day, it occurred to me that when I had been lecturing at different venues and was describing my personal stories of the icons I either co-starred with or just knew very well, the audience's reactions were very similar to that of my luncheon companion. It was then that I seriously considered trying to write a book.

The initial experience was quite eerie because, after I had written for a very short while, the memories started flooding in like a tap turned on full force. It was almost like someone else was writing the book for me; at times, it was hard just trying to keep up with the stories that were coming to my mind nonstop!

This was one surprised novice author when the five-star reviews of *My Fifteen Minutes* started coming in. They were all wonderful, but I was particularly grateful for the one that Mr. Leonard Maltin, the foremost Hollywood authority and historian, wrote, and for the extremely generous reviews that my fellow author Laura Wagner gave to me. Up until then, I had no idea that she also happened to be the book reviewer for *Classic Images*, a magazine devoted to the Golden Age of Hollywood, and read with awe when she and *Classic Images* named *My Fifteen Minutes* Best Book of 2005! Of course, just like in the profession of acting, one is always humbled by the praises of one's contemporaries and the same goes for the writing profession. I cannot forget the generosity of some of the very talented authors who gave me a thumbs-up review for my book and those thanks go to Sandra Grabman, Richard Grudens, Scott O'Brien, Robert Daniels, good pal Janet Gari (Eddie Cantor's daughter) and Bob King, editor and general manager of *Classic Images*.

I must admit that as exciting as all of this was—and it was—I was not emotionally in the best phase of my life. I had lost a lot of enthusiasm for things and events that Tony and I used to enjoy together because now he was no longer by my side and nothing was the same. Nothing. Friends and family were quite worried about this unrecognizable Sybil that no longer displayed the child-like enthusiasm she had for everything in general for most of her life. However, I don't want anyone to get the wrong impression. I did not go around in a depressed state and could still smile at the crazy things that can happen in life, but as a whole I was not the participant that I used to be on a daily basis.

South African school chums attending one of my appearances in Hollywood 2007
Geraldine and Joe Malamad. Joe is jeweler to many Hollywood stars.

As time went on, I could almost hear my dear husband scolding me and saying, "Snap out of it, Syb. You've got to get on with Life," and I just knew that he would not approve of what was happening to me. I was going to have to change and I would...but it was going to take time.

Months later, I woke up one morning feeling very restless. Ben Ohmart was still asking me for a second book, but I was totally convinced that I was a one-book author and really didn't think I could nudge any more memories of the past that I had not already done in *My Fifteen Minutes*. However, Ben asked me to give it another try and the more that I thought about it, the more I came to the conclusion that there was no harm to at least give it a go.

The next morning I took the cover off my computer, settled back and waited for the memories to come. For three or four days, staring at the keys in front of me, I waited and waited and waited, and ultimately came up...with a blank!!

Not realizing that this was a common malady that all writers experience every now and again, I heaved a sigh and emailed Ben that I just didn't have a second book in me. Much like Gary Heckman when he approached me about starting a fan club for me, Ben told me not to jump the gun, but to take a break from it and pick it up some other time. After all, the clock was not ticking toward a deadline and I must admit that that took the pressure off me.

Two weeks later, I attended a birthday party for one of my contemporaries. Since all of the guests knew each other quite well, the dialogue was free-flowing, and, eventually, everyone was telling lots of "on-the-set" stories. Pretty soon, I was doing the same and by the next day I got started on my second book, *Five Minutes More*. This really was a surprise turnaround for me because after having been convinced that one couldn't squeeze blood out of a turnip—and I was sure that my turnip had been squeezed to a dry pulp—I was amazed at what finally came forth! The

Me and President of the international Sybil Jason Fan Club, Gary Heckman, 1984.

memories did *not* come as easily as they had for my first book, but they *did* come with a little more effort and a strong hunch that Tony was right beside me prodding me into action!

After Ben had published *Five Minutes More*, it also received some wonderful five-star reviews, with the added bonus and honor of Leonard Maltin writing the foreword to my new book. I knew, without a doubt, that now my career as a writer had come to its conclusion because I was completely "tapped out" memory wise. I emailed Ben and told him what fun it had been. I couldn't have asked for a nicer publisher and wished him and BearManor Media the best of luck in all of their future endeavors. I heard from Ben and he graciously accepted my decision, but said that his door was always open to anything that I might want to write.

The writing did stop, but I had the added thrill of going on book-signing venues and meeting so many interesting people, mostly movie buffs. When they found out that I was the same person that they saw in my Warner Bros. movies showing on TCM (Turner Classic Movies) and that I was also the little character Becky in Fox's *The Little Princess*, they just wanted to settle in for the day. It was a fun experience, from both sides of the table, and it was an equal thrill when some of my neighboring fellow celebrity authors were stars that I had never met before and were now meeting on a new level as fellow writers.

One of my fondest memories after Ben had published *Five Minutes More* was that I had done the whole book on a newly acquired computer. I wasn't sure whether I was more proud of the contents of that book or that I had finally conquered the basics of the computer world!! Which leads me into the fun and light side of computers called "surfing." Just recently, I was in the midst of doing some research and in the interim came across a fascinating article written a few months ago by a South African author by the name of Ross Dix-Peek. The subject of his article was Hollywood's South African-born actors of the 1930s and 1940s. He broke it down into segments and featured Basil Rathbone, Glynis Johns, Sybil Jason, Ian Hunter, Cecil Kellaway and Louis Hayward. He was most complimentary to all of us in his individual mini-biographies of us, but what got my attention is what he wrote at the end of his article: "So when your eyes alight on South Africa's golden girl, Charlize Theron, please spare a thought for those other South African denizens of the Silver Screen who, during the '30s and '40s not only wooed countess fans but upheld South Africa's name with pride. Here's to the intrepid South African-born film pioneers of the 1930s and 1940s and may their names live forever more."

What a lovely tribute, one that I will always treasure, especially because just about everyone that he named I knew very well, with the exception of the very talented Glynis Johns, whom, regrettably, I have never met. And, now, here is the South African I knew best, as we made three movies together. Well…two and a quarter movies, anyway.

Ian Hunter

I'm sure most of you remember this fine actor and have enjoyed his performances in many a movie. Somehow, he never reached the heights of stardom that was accorded to his contemporaries like Clark Gable, Errol Flynn, and Cary Grant. However, he was always in much demand by producers and directors because they knew he would add a solid dimension to their productions, so it was a rare occasion that he was out of work.

Ian and I had much in common. If one was not familiar with either one of our careers, one might rightly assume that we were contemporaries. As Eliza Doolittle would succinctly remark, "Not bloody likely!!"

We were both born in Cape Town, South Africa, and landed up in London, England, eventually progressing to Hollywood, California, to enjoy busy and productive careers in the movies…that's where the comparisons end. By the time Ian and I were cast for the first time in the same movie, *I Found Stella Parish*, at Warner Bros. in 1935, he was a handsome six-footer with brown hair and expressive blue eyes, impeccable manners (both on and off the screen) and was 35 years old. I was Warner Bros.' first child star and was seven years old! (*I Found Stella Parish* was my second film at Warners; my first was *Little Big Shot*.)

Our boss, Mr. Jack Warner, was a devoted Anglophile and liked nothing better than to team up his Brit discoveries as much as possible and there were many of us under his banner both before and behind the camera. The ones who had the most difficult time of it were his writers, who had the difficult task of explaining away British accents that were out of place amongst a cast of mainly American actors and actresses. Some of the explanations they used really did stretch the limits of the imaginations of the movie-going public, but somehow the audiences accepted them with good grace.

To give you an example of this, I turn to the Warner Bros. 1937 movie *The Great O'Malley* (where unbelievably I was credited *above* Humphrey Bogart). I still had a major English accent, but because the wonderful character actress Frieda Inescort, who portrayed my mother, was originally from Scotland and had a "cultured" accent, we "fit" and it was easily accepted. However, cast as my daddy was Bogey, who even then had a movie reputation as a tough guy and solid American. It was hard to swallow that the three of us fit as a family and shared the same background. Due to a throwaway line that the writers put into the script, the explanation for our accents was that we all came from Canada!! Canadians must have had a good laugh at that one when the movie was shown there!

By the time I was making *I Found Stella Parish*, which starred Kay Francis and cast Ian as her leading man (the first of seven movies they did together), the writers didn't even try to explain away our various accents. In the storyline, although Kay's character was an American, she was a major star on the British stage for a number of years and Ian was a reporter on a London newspaper.

In *Five Minutes More*, I tried to give a rundown of what usually happens on the first morning of a new production. Most of the time the stars and supporting players arrive on the set prepared with memorized dialogue scheduled for that day and to hear from our director and to go through the storyline thoroughly. One might think that this would be superfluous, seeing that we probably had our scripts for a few weeks prior to shooting our first scene. Unlike stage productions, movies are not shot in sequence. On the first day of shooting one might do a scene that takes place in the middle of the story or, as sometimes happens (but thankfully not that often), the last scene in the movie! After all of the discussions have taken place, the actors go through the physical motions of the scene, making sure that they hit their marks so that they don't get out of camera range and that they stay within their key lighting while the director and the cinematographer work hand in hand supervising the scene camera-wise. It's then that the stand-ins take our places so that the gaffers (the lighting men) can adjust all of the lights for the best possible results, which sometimes can take an inordinate amount of time for various technical reasons. When that happens, it gives the actors a lot of free time to relax, socialize, or just get in some quiet time for themselves. It wasn't that simple for me. By law, I had to get in at least three hours of school work daily and the only way in which that could be accomplished was by bits and pieces. The teacher would log me in and then log me out of my scenes and by the time midday approached and I had not reached at least halfway through my three hours, lawfully the teacher could shut the set down and that could cost the production a lot of money, especially if the kid star was in most of the scenes of the movie. But, even with all that, there was still time left over that did allow the cast to socialize, which in a way helped to enhance our screen performances. I, naturally, bonded with Kay Francis because she looked like my own mother and was very loving and supportive of me in countless ways.

Ian, my sister Anita and I spent a lot of time together mainly discussing and updating our fellow South African on our mutual birth town. Although Ian was born in Cape Town, he and his family had moved to London when he was just a teenager. Although he remembered the physicality of South Africa, and especially Cape Town, he was extremely interested in us giving him updated information in a generalized way.

Ian had a lovely subdued sense of humor and was extremely easy to work with. Anita and he compared notes about the people that all of us dealt with business-wise in London, like Irving Asher, who was the head of the London division of Warner Bros. studios. Irving was, in most cases, directly responsible for suggesting who would be best considered for a Hollywood contract and, for the most part, his recommendations were taken seriously in Hollywood. I know that Errol Flynn and I were signed at the same time and brought over to Hollywood by Jack Warner and Hal Wallis.

The years at Warner Bros. were busy and productive ones, but, as sometimes happens in Hollywood (and still does), a mere two years' time makes a huge difference.

By 1938, Kay Francis, who was considered Warner Bros. top leading lady and box-office champ, was delegated to unfortunate roles by the studio. They had been grooming Bette Davis to take her place and she was given first consideration for the plum movie productions. One of those less-than-first-rate productions was *Comet Over Broadway* (originally named *Curtain Call*, a better title) and teamed Kay, Ian and myself once again. We all felt the crunch and although my first Warner Bros. director, Michael Curtiz, was supposed to have directed this soap opera, he was replaced by my former dance director (and uncredited director of the musical sequences starring Al Jolson and myself in *The Singing Kid*), the genius Busby Berkeley. Curtiz, years later, did a beautiful job of direction on the musical *Yankee Doodle Dandy*. In comparison and in reverse, I don't think that Buz, at that time, really understood the genre of drama. Years later, he did, but not on *Comet Over Broadway*, which deservedly bombed at the box office and put an end to some careers at Warner Bros., including mine.

The next time I saw Ian was a year later when I was signed to a contract at 20th Century-Fox and we were assigned to the same movie. Yes, this was our third movie, but incongruously he and I never had one scene together in *The Little Princess*, which starred Shirley Temple. He played Shirley's father and I portrayed the little cockney scullery maid Becky in the exclusive school that Shirley attended while her father went off to war…in South Africa.

Many things had changed for all of us (including Shirley, who was "maturing"), and, sadly, I don't think that Ian and I exchanged but a few words during the whole production. Realistically, the reason for that was that when I was working in my scenes he was not…and when he was working, I was not!

I must say that many, many years later I watched, in awe, some of the movies that Ian did in London. He had developed into a fine character actor with depths he never got to explore in his Hollywood career, but he certainly made up for it in his mature years.

About Your 8x10

There is a very funny story attached to your photo. It was one of many publicity stills that were taken in between shooting scenes for our movie *I Found Stella Parish*.

In the 8x10 you see me and Ian Hunter, who was also born in Cape Town, South Africa. I hadn't been in America too long and was still very, very British and there were some things about the American slang terms I didn't understand. When our cameraman asked me to give Ian a smack, I was just horrified!! However, as I was taught to always follow directions, I gently faked giving Ian a slap on the cheek. Imagine my surprise when both men burst out laughing after the picture was taken. You see, the American term for giving a kiss was "a smack," but, being the new Brit in town, a smack, to me, only meant one thing…a slap on the face!!

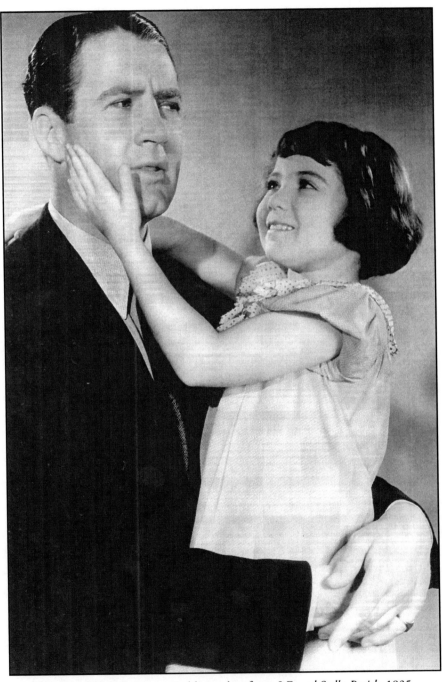

The famous "slap" picture. Publicity shot from *I Found Stella Parish*, 1935.
Ian Hunter and me

By the way, the other photograph with Ian and I took place on board ship and the lady directly behind me in the deck chair, Jessie Ralph, who played my nanny in *I Found Stella Parish*, just four years later played the fairy godmother to Shirley in our movie, *The Blue Bird*.

Shuffleboard scene of me and Ian Hunter from *I Found Stella Parish*, 1935.
In back of me on deck chair is Jessie Ralph.

Guy Kibbee & May Robson

When I started writing this newsletter for my fan club, I was going to go for generalizations rather than specifics like I usually did, such as featuring stories about one specific star. Somehow, my brain was given a bit of a nudge and my memory automatically beamed its way into a movie that I did in 1936 at Warner Bros. called *The Captain's Kid*. It starred, as billed, May Robson, me, and Guy Kibbee.

I knew immediately that I would have absolutely no trouble coming up with some amusing things that happened while making that movie. So, the following was what I started to write…but, as you will soon see, after a few pages, I put my mental brakes on, changed in midstream and featured two wonderful actors who added dimension to every movie they ever appeared in. Hopefully, you will indulge me in my flip-flop action for I can assure you that I have deleted nothing because I have incorporated what I initially wrote and then segued into my personal profile of those two adorable scene-stealers… Ms. May Robson and Mr. Guy Kibbee.

[*Note*: The newsletter did not have this picture of me and Mr. Kibbee, even though I had mentioned what a terrific whittler of wood he was. However, since then, I have come across a picture with us in it and, if you look very closely, you will see the formation of my head and body that he was producing from that block of wood. How I wish that I still had it.]

About Your 8x10

This photo was taken during the making of *The Captain's Kid* in 1936 at Warner Bros. studio and let me tell you that we three "kids" (Kibbee, Robson and Jason) had a marvelous time throughout the whole production. Age related, I may have been the youngest of the three, but

Guy Kibbee carving my form out of block of wood.

their enthusiasm for life in general had no boundaries, no expiration date, and, best of all, none of us experienced one iota of age disparity. We were all on an even keel!

On our first day of shooting, Mr. Kibbee, who was an incredible wood whittler, started off with a plain block of wood that was approximately 12 inches long and 8 inches wide. He always worked on it in between scenes and even on camera and, magically, by the time the production had come to an end, that shapeless piece of wood had emerged as a fully-formed replica of me from head to foot!! I kept that loving piece of art work for years, but, much to my sorrow, somewhere down the line while traveling from South Africa back to the USA after World War II, it got lost in transit.

In regards to Mr. Kibbee's role in *The Captain's Kid,* it was similar to the one he did at Fox's in *Captain January,* starring Shirley Temple, and he was marvelous in both of them. One of the things that delighted him on our movie was when his beautiful little adopted daughter, Shirley Ann Kibbee, came to visit our set and he made arrangements with our still photographer to take a picture of both Shirley and me. When he saw a print of it later on, he remarked that he would always treasure the picture that showed "both of his girls" together.

One of the many fun things that we did was going on location to Long Beach where, in the movie, "Uncle Asa" had a boat. As is very often the case, there are long periods of waiting in between scenes for various technical reasons. When that happened, Mr. Kibbee, who was an avid fisherman, got out his fishing gear and started fishing off the dock. I watched him in fascination and told him I had never gone fishing in my life and it sure looked like fun. Making sure that that little detail would be taken care of immediately, he made sure that I had a hat to protect me from the sun and then asked one of the crew to please find me a small fishing pole. That was one of the most fun adventures I ever had as a kid and, on top of it all, I caught my first fish! What I didn't know until years

Getting my first fishing lesson.

Visitor on set Shirley Ann Kibbee.

later was that Mr. Kibbee had paid one the crew members to dive under where we were fishing and to put a fish on my hook!!!! I even have home movies of me bringing up that wiggling fish.

There were some other very amusing things that happened on that movie of ours. I have to set up the scene for you so that you can properly imagine what happened that led up to a great deal of laughing from all of us.

It is a scene where our family chauffer has an altercation with some thieves in a hotel room. They knock the chauffer out with a blow to the head and in the interim I am trying to get away and get some help for him. I run to the outside of the hotel and get into our limousine that is parked in front of the hotel and I start the car. By this time, the chauffer staggers out of the hotel and joins me in the car where a chase ensues and the thieves are following us in their car. When the chauffer passes out once again, I take over the wheel until he comes to again and you see me standing up in the car telling him how close the other car is getting to us. Toward the end of the chase, he brings our car safely to a halt while the other car crashes into a hillside. There was a lot of stunt driving during that sequence and, naturally, the studio was not going to take any chances of me getting hurt so they decided to use a double for me.

By the next day, wardrobe and makeup had duplicated my dress, my coat, my Mary Jane shoes, my dressy straw hat and underneath the hat was a fantastic wig that looked just like my signature Dutch bob. Now, my double was all set to take my place in the car. When the double stepped into the scene, cast and crew just lost it and broke up uncontrollably at the sight of what they saw. My double was a gentleman "midget" who had incredibly hairy legs that peeked out of the duplications of my very girly clothes. It took some while for everyone to settle down before they could get back to work, but that dear man displayed a lot of class and good humor and just simply ignored the chaos that he had caused and never, in any way, retaliated…not once! The crew must have felt badly about how they had reacted because later in the day they all pitched in and got him a case of beer!!!

May Robson

During the making of *The Captain's Kid*, I was a most fortunate young actress in that I adored Guy Kibbee and loved working with him, yet I had the same feelings toward May Robson. Our close relationship was very much like I had with my own grandmother when I stayed in her home in London before I came to Hollywood.

She and I talked a lot in between scenes and in one of our conversations I had mentioned how much I loved my pets, Mr. McTavish, a scotty dog (Mac for short), and Peter, a wirehaired terrier. After our movie was finished, I had the pleasure of visiting Miss Robson in her home. I was awestruck when I saw that she had the largest collection of birds and aviary of any one private person in the United States at that

Captains Kid. Scene she giving me knitting lessons.

time. This amazing "young" lady had many interests, and acting was just one of them.

One day, on the set, a gentleman knocked on my trailer dressing room door and delivered a small basket which was topped with a pretty pink blanket. I no sooner had reached to pull off the blanket when it moved and out popped the head of the sweetest black Siamese kitten. It was a present from Miss Robson and it didn't take me but a few minutes to decide on the kitten's name. I named her Muzzy May, which was Miss Robson's own nickname, and, I swear, from day one, that little kitten thought she was a dog. She, Mac and Peter got along so well that they all ate out of the same bowl at mealtimes and it was more than heartwarming that her "brothers" were always so protective of her.

There are some things in show business that are quite incongruous and are hard to explain and this next story is one of them.

Some of you young readers may not recognize May Robson by name, but, if you are a true movie buff and tune into TCM, you will easily recognize her from her many roles in major motion pictures. One of her unforgettable performances was in a Warner Bros. movie starring the Lane sisters, John Garfield, and Claude Rains, *Four Daughters*. She was magnificent in it, but, as so often happens in Hollywood, she lost out in *The Hollywood Reporter* poll as best supporting actress of 1939 to…my performance as Becky in 20th Century-Fox's *The Little Princess*! Life is certainly stranger than fiction!

Throughout most of *The Captain's Kid*, May's character was forever harping at Mr. Kibbee's character for one thing or another. Actually, they loved each other and had been sweethearts when they were young, but never married due to his overwhelming interest in following up on ancient treasure maps and looking for gold and jewels.

"Uncle Asa" had always been my hero and I was prone to sticking up for him and telling white lies to protect him. Therefore, in the interim, I become a handful and land him in jail. In the courtroom scene, when it was obvious that I was telling a bunch of lies, May gets up and puts me over her knee and gives me a good spanking. (I have to smile nowadays when I see that several people on YouTube felt that that scene was definitely in the realm of child abuse!!) Actually, the fact of the matter was, the director was planning on having a book or magazine placed inside my panties to protect me from the spanking, but my sister and I both agreed it would look more natural if my rear end was not protected; my reactions would be true to life. May was not happy with this decision, but we followed through with it and the results were very good judging by the comments on YouTube in this day and age and the reviews of the movie when it was released.

Several of the reviewers then (and movie historians nowadays) have mentioned that there never has been as dramatic crying scene from a child star as there was from me in the jail scene in *The Captain's Kid*. I must admit that although *The Captain's Kid* is a well done, but very "light" piece of entertainment, I am most proud of that scene than on any other

Reality...*me* giving *her* knitting lessons.

dramatic moments that I may have had on the more prestigious movies that I was privileged to be in.

Between May's character's continually harping at Asa and me being spanked by her, our director, Nick Grinde, also wanted to show the very gentle side of her (which actually was the dominant side of her). He had her sitting in a wing chair in her living room calmly knitting a garment. Abigail (me) had a habit of running away from home and joining Uncle Asa wherever he was, but her aunt (May) was secure in the feeling that she was safely tucked away in bed and could not join Asa because he was now in jail.

The scene was set up and the prop man handed May a swatch of knitting along with knitting needles and yarn and Mr. Grinde ordered the scene to begin. It wasn't long before the director called a halt to the shoot and directed Miss Robson to give more "energy" to the business of knitting. They started once again, but once again the director called "CUT" and asked, "May, is there a problem with the action?" In a very embarrassed voice, May Robson announced, "I don't know *how* to knit!" It had been wrongly assumed that a lady of her age certainly knew how to knit. Not deterred by her answer, Mr. Grinde asked, "Is there anyone here on the set that could coach Miss Robson just enough to give the *impression* that she really is knitting?" Going outside of the set to find a knitter would just waste time, so he was hoping someone on site could do the job. Unfortunately, there were no volunteers, but, suddenly, the silence was broken by a small voice saying, "I can knit, Mr. Grinde." It was me. Those of you who have read my two last books will recall that when I was five years old my grandmother in England taught me how to knit and I used the expertise in Hollywood by knitting a scarf (when I first arrived in America) for my big crush, the original "blue eyes," Dick Powell. Miss Robson was a fast learner and, in a very short while, managed to look like an experienced knitter.

Filmmakers, then and now, are notorious pranksters and our crew did not let an opportunity go by to make sure that the beloved actress May Robson would not forget that she was "coached in acting" by a five-year-old child! Therefore, on the last day of the film, we had an on-set party with food galore and we all exchanged gifts to each other. There was this one particularly large box which was beautifully wrapped for Miss Robson and, after she made a lot of oohs and aahs over the wrappings, she finally opened the box. When she saw the contents, she let out a huge guffaw!! I'm sure you must have guessed by now that the box contained multiple knitting instruction books, tons of skeins of wool, different-sized knitting needles and a beautiful sewing basket to contain all those items. With a twinkle in her eyes, she good-naturedly said, "I'll have you jokesters know that I'm going to put all of this to bloody good use!!" Her speech was met with a big round of applause and, knowing Miss Robson, I bet she did…and did it expertly!!

Rudy Vallee

About Your 8x10

This was taken in the living room of my first Hollywood home. Before arriving in Hollywood, I had done a guest shot on the Rudy Vallee radio show in New York in 1935. After the show, he signed this photo for me which I treasured because it was my first autographed picture from an American celebrity. As a crooner, Rudy led the way for the Sinatras, the Crosbys, and so many other singers that came after his tremendous success as a star vocalist. His records sold like hotcakes and when he had his own radio show in New York, it became so popular that he had no trouble securing top celebrities as his guest stars. In time, he relocated to Hollywood and combined singing with acting in motion pictures. Rudy was a guest in my home on several occasions and many years later, when I was an adult, we attended a small banquet at Warner Bros. studios.

In the thirties, apart from my work day schedule on the lot or appearances arranged by the studio, one actually did have time to socialize in our homes. My sister Anita, my uncle Harry and I either had small gatherings attended by stars who were very good friends or larger parties that included other stars and musicians who we were reciprocating for past invitations that were extended to us to their homes.

We had a very large three-story house on Sunset Boulevard, so were not restricted by space. However, everyone seemed to congregate to our living room where we were fortunate that our very dear and close friend, musical genius and composer Johnny Green, whose songs included "Body and Soul" and "I Cover the Waterfront," would sit down at the piano and thoroughly entertain everyone by playing the popular songs of the day.

Me with my first American star autograph (1935) in Hollywood. *Inset:* At Warner Bros studio (approx 1950) at banquet honoring Jane Wyman and myself.

Sometimes some of our famous singing star guests would get up and sing along with what Johnny was playing.

Years later, Johnny Green became musical director at MGM studios and became an Oscar winner for his music in the movie *Oliver!*

Just to give you an idea what it was like, our parties were very relaxed, so much so that many of our closest friends were free to wander around the house. Loveable Pat O'Brien almost always wandered into the kitchen, much to the delight of our help. They just adored him as he would sample just about everything that was to be put out later for our guests to eat and would comment favorably on each and every tidbit. Because of his natural warmth, he never forgot to ask how their kids were doing in school and what their interests were now that the kids were older. He wouldn't rush his visit to the kitchen, but it never failed that, before he left to rejoin the rest of the guests, he would always leave some money for our help in a place that they would find later on. Pat was always Mr. Generosity, but never made a big thing of it.

And talking about generosity in the reverse...we get to our main subject...Rudy Vallee. Rudy was one of the funniest guests we ever had. As I have already told you in *My Fifteen Minutes*, before my guardians and I arrived in Hollywood, we had a brief stay of four days in New York after our ship landed from England. Warners had arranged to have us escorted all around town. It was an exciting time for us to visit all of the wondrous landmarks in that city and part of the itinerary also included for me to appear as a guest star on the Rudy Vallee radio show.

We now jump in time to a couple of years later. By this time, Warners had established me in the eyes of the public as their own child star by starring me in a few movies and now here we all were in Hollywood, including Rudy, who had relocated to the west coast. By now, this singing icon had attended quite a few parties in my home. Although he was always welcome, he did have a strange idiosyncrasy. It was no secret that Rudy Vallee was richer by far than most of the stars in Hollywood at that time, but it was also a known fact that as a guest in your home he had the reputation of having a slight case of "sticky fingers." We found that out the very first time he came to our house.

In those days when everyone smoked, it was par for the course to have sterling silver cigarette boxes strategically placed around the living room where guests were welcome to partake of the cigarettes in case they had run out of their own or had just forgotten to bring some. Without even trying to be unobtrusive about it, Rudy used to take not just one or two cigarettes, but would grab a whole fistful of them and put them in his pocket! This did not come as a surprise to us because we had been forewarned to be aware that this kind of thing would happen and to be on the lookout for what he would choose as his prize for the evening. It was never anything expensive, so it was not a matter of stealing, but it did provide the Hollywood crowd a great deal of entertainment trying to guess what his target of the night would be!!!

Many, many years later it seems that his cautious ways with a dollar had not changed. He had the reputation of never picking up a check at a restaurant for more people than just he and his wife. Even when it was just the two of them, he would peruse each item on the bill for an absurd amount of time before reluctantly paying it.

Around this time, Warner Bros. was holding a small banquet to honor Jane Wyman and me at the studio and as happens occasionally at some events, other than the honorees, the other guests picked up the tab for their own meals. I was sitting next to Rudy and his lovely wife and when most people had almost finished their meal, Rudy noticed that there was still a lot of food left on his wife's plate. He cautioned her, "Finish it all up. We *paid* for this meal!" To some of you this may sound like he was a mean man, but he was anything but. He was very sweet and his idiosyncrasy never stopped anyone from inviting him to their home, for everyone felt that he was well worth any little "token" he would take. That evening at Warners was the last time that I saw Rudy, but as you can see by the snapshot he looked very well and happy.

The Media

About Your 8x10

I'm sure that you recognize that your autographed photograph is from the movie *The Little Princess*. However, I don't think you realize that this is a rare photo because it was shot *after* Shirley and I did the scene. As characters in the movie, we had just discovered wonderful food, warm clothing and a roaring fire in the fireplace in Sara's (Shirley's) cold, damp

Shirley Temple, and me *Little Princess* and famous muffin story.

room. Poor little Becky (me) spots her favorite food (muffins) and, as directed, begins to stuff her mouth full of them.

In the movie, you never really get to see how many I actually ate, but I'll tell you right now it was always two or three at a time. Not so bad, you say? Try doing this for the camera four times!!! In your photo, note the expressions on our faces. She is about to break up in a fit of giggles and I've got a kind of sickly grin on my face after we had just been told that they were playing a joke on me and that the first take was perfect!! I had just ingested a minimum of eight muffins, needlessly, but, believe it or not, I still love them to this day.

Do not feel sorry for me, though. The director, Walter Lang, was a good friend of my sister's and me and this joke was not meant in a mean way. In fact,, it gave me a lot of laughs for years to come just thinking about it.

I have discovered that throughout the years movie buffs have an insatiable appetite for any story that involves Shirley Temple and myself. For the *true* fans who love the two movies that we did together, *The Little Princess and The Blue Bird*, it unfailingly brings smiles to their faces and compliments galore.

However, and thankfully it's only occasionally, it's a different story when it comes to the media and some authors who strive for a different slant on our relationship, whether true or false.

I will never forget one writer who came to my home to interview me. Before we got started, he asked if I minded if he tape recorded me. I have never minded being tape recorded, so I agreed and we soon started the Q&A session. Everything went along nicely until we got to the topic of Shirley. He became insistent about any conflicts or jealousies we might have had for each other. I told him that, whether onscreen or off, we got along beautifully, but I could tell that didn't seem to satisfy him. Almost immediately, he rephrased the question. For all intents and purposes, the question was the same, and...so was the answer. Calling upon all of his self-control, he suggested that we might take a break. I agreed and after some pleasantries, coffee and cake, we resumed the interview. He started off asking me about my time at Warner Bros. and about some of my famous co-stars. It did not take long before he was back to Shirley and the supposed "tensions and jealousies we suffered" toward each other. Calling upon *my* self-control, I looked him straight in the eye and, very slowly and precisely, gave him my same answer for the *third* time! He gave me a very weak smile, switched off his recorder and thanked me for my hospitality and left my home. I'll give the gentleman points for the very nice article he wrote about me, but, surprisingly, Shirley and our two movies were never mentioned!

It was not only authors or magazine writers that wrote apocryphal tales about the stars that the public tended to believe. Each studio had

Feature story of top child stars of the thirties. Me in middle picture.
(*Chicago Tribune*)

Me and Jackie Cooper at book signing 2009.

their publicity departments and their main purpose was to keep their contract players in the eyes of the public as much as possible, even if they fed the public the truth, half-truths or out-and-out fairy tales that only existed in the minds of the people who worked for their studios' publicity departments.

When Shirley Temple and I were making *The Little Princess* in 1939, Fox's publicity department had a lot of fuel to ignite and cause interest in their pending production that starred Shirley. They were quick to point out that this would be Shirley's very first Technicolor movie (true) and she would be supported by a top-flight cast (true). They also put to rest the rumor that Mrs. Gertrude Temple would not have Sybil Jason in a movie alongside her daughter Shirley. (It may have been initially true, but that rumor was proved false with the advent of *The Little Princess*.) Fox publicity took every chance they had of reminding the public about this fact and how very well the two little actresses got along together (true).

When they ran dry to keep the public apprised of the newest facts from their production of *The Little Princess*, they resorted to half-truths. Supposedly, in between scenes, when Shirley and I were sitting in our

Jackie Cooper and me at historic radio broadcast to Buenos Aries 1936.

director's chairs waiting to go into our next scene, a woman's scream was heard. The trade papers wrote in the very next day's issues that Shirley and I narrowly escaped possible death or disfigurement when red-hot carbon used in the back of the large arc lights fell from one of the catwalks and

PROBLEM PICTURE We put this in for fear you might be tired of all the love stuff Among those present are Leo Carrillo, Merle Oberon, Francis Lederer, Olivia De Havilland, Jeanette MacDonald, Gene Raymond, Anita Louise, Jackie Cooper and Sybil Jason. Try and identify them in sixty seconds

Lineup of stars at broadcast to Buenos Aries. (*left to right*) Ceo representative of Buenos Aries, Merle Oberon, Olivia De Havilland (*back row*) Francis Lederer, Front MC Leo Carrillo, (Back row) Anita Louise (*front row*) Sybil Jason, Jackie Cooper, Jeanette McDonald, Gene Raymond. (*back row unknown*)

barely missed hitting us. It was noted that time out was called "so that the two little girls could get over their scare." First of all, Shirley was in her trailer dressing room and I was sitting in the area where I used to do my school work. The poor person that almost got hit by the red-hot carbon was my dear sister Anita. Both Cesar Romero and Anita Louise rushed to her side to see that she was all right (true).

That wasn't the only thing that Anita escaped from that was written up for the trades by the Fox publicity machine. They mentioned that the parrot that was used by Cesar Romero in several scenes was pretty mean and during one sequence flew off camera and bit Shirley's stand-in's finger (false). The parrot *was* mean and the bird *did* bite a finger, but that of Anita and not Shirley's stand-in!! Of course, that wouldn't have made for any kind of "drama" to present to the public, so they resorted to a "fairy tale."

Other than that, Shirley and I escaped completely from any hazardous misadventure during the shooting of *The Little Princess*, but poor Anita couldn't say the same!!

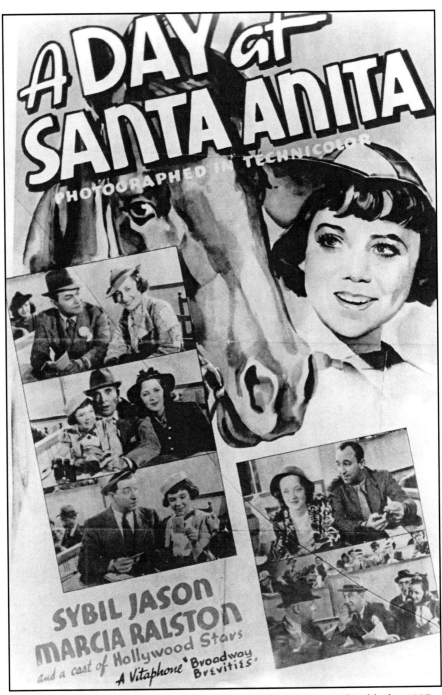

Poster of my Warner Bros technicolor short w.guest stars pictured in blocks, 1937.
Edward G. Robinson, Olivia De Havilland, Al Jolson, Ruby Keeler, Frank McHugh,
Bette Davis, Alan Jenkins, Joseph Creehan, Hugh Herbert.

Little Big Book featuring me in my first Warner Bros movie *Little Big Shot*.

Nothing too much has changed in this era. These same kinds of stories are written up every day and they do accomplish what they set out to do: to keep their clients in the eye of the public at all costs. So do be wary of everything you read. Not everything is written in stone!!

Me digging first spadeful for new Warner Bros Theatre, Shaker Heights,Ohio. 1937.
Pictured behind my left shoulder my bodyguard Eliot Ness, 2nd from left Mayor
ofCleveland, the rest...Warner Bros CEO'S.

Freddie Bartholemew's birthday at MGM. (*in dark on left back*) Dickie Moore,
Bonita Granville and Judy Garland, (*front*) Tommy Kelly and Sybil Jason.

Will Hollywood History Repeat Itself?

There is a theory that we experience the same things in life over and over again, century after century. Although it's sometimes called deja vu or even reincarnation, in either case we rarely recognize it as such. Perhaps that's the very reason we have such a hard time finding solutions to the problems that exist today because we view them as newly formed and not a repeat of the past in which these specific problems have been solved.

In 1933, the unemployment in America was without precedence and took root in 1929 as the Great Depression. It took a stranglehold on the American public and up until then this nation was always considered a privileged society by the rest of the world. But, to the horror of the men who headed the American family, middle class suddenly became the poor and the breadwinners found themselves not the mainstay of their families but as nonentities standing in bread lines so that their wives and children could eat for at least one day at a time. This was a time before President Roosevelt initiated the Social Security Act, which later on gave a certain amount of security month to month to those who were unemployed.

As bad as all of this was, some families managed to eke out just enough money to attend some form of entertainment as an escape from the reality of their lives. The parks were still free and so were the libraries and if one was fortunate enough to own a radio, the whole family could be entertained weekly by the stars of comedy, drama, and song. But the best escape of all was motion pictures.

For an hour and a half, a family could physically get away from their drab home life and sink into the luxurious carpeting and upholstered chairs of the movie theatres and admire the glamorous stars of that day and vicariously live an uncomplicated life for an hour or two. So what if

41

one had to choose whether to have a sparse dinner or pay the admittance to a movie theatre? The choice was not hard for most people. They figured that what little food that they had on hand would only last a few minutes and if they forfeited another trip to the grocery store and instead paid for their tickets to the movies that would be their Great Escape and the family could extend the enjoyment by discussing what they had just seen when they got home after the show.

There is a fashion fad that I must admit I take no pleasure in our present-day society. It's seeing young people paying horrendous prices for carefully torn-up jeans as a fashion statement. During the Depression, a lot of kids were ashamed to go to school because they had tears in their clothing due to usage and their mothers went to great lengths to try to mend the garments so that their kids' clothes didn't scream poverty. However, some of their schoolmates were quite cruel and the less fortunate were made fun of, which, in turn caused a lack of self-confidence that carried well over into adulthood. Instead of the carefree innocence of youth that kids are entitled to, they prematurely carried the problems of lack on their shoulders.

In spite of the bread lines, unemployment, and everything that one had to face during the Great Depression, Hollywood provided a shining light that infiltrated the gloom families had to deal with on a daily basis and the name of this small miracle was a dimpled darling named Shirley Temple. She was a multi-talented child who represented, in all of her innocence and vitality, a hope for the future. That hope took some time in coming, but for an hour's time, up on the screen, during the thirties, one could forget the outside world and encompass themselves in this child's optimistic world. Her popularity was unprecedented up until that time. Even though other equally talented children earned their place in the sun as popular child stars of the thirties and forties, Shirley always held her number-one position. Being quite realistic, I was never jealous of her standing in world popularity because I realized for those of us that came within Shirley's sphere there was enough faithful followers that attended our movies and kept us up on that screen long enough so that, to this present day, fan mail and fan clubs still exist for a lot of us.

Now, in 2009 America, the world is suffering through another Depression. Although the big movie moneymakers for quite a number of years have been the horror movies and extravaganzas like the *Superman, Star Trek* and *Star Wars* movies, I wonder if it's also the time to backtrack to a more innocent time in the form of another child star who would represent everything good that we want in our lives and in the lives of our children? Or have we become such a disillusioned and hard-bitten society that we might snicker at the purity of the innocence that a child star would offer us? I am afraid of the answer to that, but I can only hope that the mothers of small children will take advantage of the reissued movies of Shirley's and of mine and other child stars of the past that would appeal to their children's interest in age-appropriate movies, which are far and few between nowadays. I do think that the men and women who are in charge of scheduling movies to be aired (some of them are comparatively young CEOs who do not recognize the names of the juvenile stars and do not program their movies) really need to brush up on their Hollywood history. One of the best is the cable network Turner Classic Movies, who, although they could do a little improving on presenting past Hollywood movies starring juveniles, certainly do a service by providing movies that very young people could understand and appreciate. Certainly, the extra bonus would be the residual appreciation of the parents who could then appreciate that a good and healthy mental element had been introduced into their children's entertainment lives. A good example of this is the *Our Gang* comedy series that is provided on a fairly regular basis on television.

Will Hollywood history repeat itself? Is there another Shirley on the horizon and, if there is, will she be accepted in this era? Only you, the public, can answer that.

Jane Wyman

About Your 8x10

I know most of you have seen all of her movies starting with the lighthearted comedies she did for Warner Bros. to the very dramatic ones she did later on. She gained the reputation on the lot as being cute as a button and, as a matter of fact, one of her boyfriends (and later her husband) gave her the nickname of Button Nose.

Jane was a warm and sweet person and extremely talented, but her talent wasn't recognized until much later on in her career. She was in an awful lot of fluff until she showed the world what she was really made of in *Johnny Belinda*, for which she won the Academy Award for Best Actress.

One of those pieces of fluff was in a Technicolor short that I starred in called *Little Pioneer*, which is still to be seen every now and again on TCM, and, I believe, shown as an extra on a Warner Bros. DVD. It never fails to happen that when people view this short they always ask who dubbed her singing voice, not realizing that at the tender age of sixteen she was a band singer.

We worked very well together and because the storyline took place in South Africa, she was fascinated that I was actually born there. She asked many questions and was very surprised to learn how modern South Africa was. At that time, all people knew of South Africa was what they saw on the travelogues, which usually just concentrated on Kruger National Park and the wild animals. Nowadays, of course, it's a different story because a lot of the studios film their movies there due to the ideal weather conditions and the beautiful and pristine locations.

Talking about locations, we shot most of that short at Sherwood Lake near Thousand Oaks in California and many years later Tony, my

Main picture from WB technicolor short *Little Pioneer,* 1938.
(*left to right*) Sybil, Jane Wyman, Carleton Moore Jr.
Inset: Jane and I being honored at Warner Bros. (approx 1950)

husband, and I climbed under the barrier so that I could show him where we shot a certain scene. Before we knew it, a police car pulled up and warned us we were trespassing on city property and, unless we wanted to pay a very heavy fine and perhaps serve jail time, we should leave immediately. When we explained what our "trespassing" was all about, his face broke out in a grin and he told us as long as we didn't venture any further and if we left as soon as possible, he would ignore our "visit." He got into his car and left us with the typical California greeting, "Have a nice day!!"

I have always admired Warner Bros. films because they made it a habit to see to the smallest details and this short was no exception. Just for the sake of realism, they imported real Cape buffalo that pulled our covered wagon in our exterior scenes and that ultimately did not go to waste as it was certainly recognized when this short played in South African theaters.

By this time, I had starred in quite a few movies for the studio and had never had any problems with either wardrobe or makeup, but, because I was a little older and they wanted me to look more like a child that came from the Boer War era, they decided I should wear a long brunette wig in place of my usual Dutch boy hairdo. From day one I always thought that the wig was not going to stay on my head. If you ever see this short, you will notice that the very nice man that portrayed Jane's father would affectionately pat my head and, when he did, I would reach up in a panic to hold onto the wig just in case!! That was my only problem on the whole shoot but...Jane had hers, too, but it was of a personal nature and quite embarrassing for both parties involved.

There was a handsome young man who was trying to court Jane and almost every day on our location schedule he would come all the way down to Sherwood Lake and visit her (pre-freeways, it was quite a journey). Every second she wasn't in front of the camera, they were never apart and that was starting to get to the director, Bobby Connolly. He felt that this young man was monopolizing Jane's time too much and that she could have put that time to better use, so he banned the very handsome young man from our location site for the rest of the shooting schedule. Of course, that didn't stop him from pursuing Jane, who he affectionately nicknamed Button Nose. He, too, was under contract to Warner Bros. and, seeing that he was on the same lot as she was, it wasn't hard for him to keep in touch with her, which he obviously did. I often wondered what happened to that fellow. His name was Ronald Reagan.

Many, many years later, when Tony and I were first married and I was doing a stage play as Dorothy in *The Wizard of Oz*, right next door to the theatre was a hotel-restaurant complex. I was taking a break from rehearsals and having lunch with Tony when who should walk in but Jane Wyman and some associates of hers. Apparently, they had driven quite a distance from out of town and decided to stop and have a bite to eat before they continued on with their journey back into California. Needless to say, after I approached her, we had a wonderful get together and, because she was interested in what had happened to me after I had done *The Little Princess* (she was so complimentary to me about my part as Becky) and *The Blue Bird* at Fox, I brought her up to date. She couldn't believe that I was now old enough to be married, but, when I introduced her to my Tony, she said that she could understand why I married so young. It was such a shame that our reunion was so short, but I had to get back to rehearsals and she and her business associates had to continue on with their journey. However, we did manage another meeting a few years after that.

Warner Bros. honored Jane and me with a small banquet held at the studio commissary, and she looked a wee bit different from the last time I had seen her at that hotel restaurant. She had let the color in her hair grow out so that now it was grey for her part in the TV series *Falcon Crest*, but she still had a young face largely due to that cute little button nose of hers. I was so sorry to have initially heard that she and Ronnie had divorced many years back because I had seen the beginnings of their romance and they had made such a cute couple, but they both had taken different roads in their lives and he, of course, became President of the United States and she continued on with her very distinguished acting career.

Welcome Back, Sybil

This next newsletter to members of my fan club has a special meaning to me and you will soon see why I will treasure it forever. It was written not by me, but by my dear husband, Anthony Drake, a mere eight months before he lost his brave and gallant battle against lung cancer. However, I am so very grateful that although this was one of the very last events that he was able to attend, he enjoyed it so very thoroughly. It was a happy event for everyone and here is his wonderful and full description of my birthday celebration that was held at Warner Bros. studio in November 2004.

Former Warner Bros. child star is rediscovered at Warner Bros. Studio. The brilliant marquee that graced the entrance to the impressively beautiful Ross Theatre on the studio lot said it all:

HAPPY BIRTHDAY
SYBIL JASON
WELCOME BACK

And what a welcome it was first for the dozens of fans who came to help Sybil celebrate, but, also, for Sybil herself, who, in the thirties, was a miniature queen on this very studio lot. The festivities all started on November 30 at the tour center and the famous Warner Bros. Museum. After all the visitors passed the stringent security checkpoint, the happy group boarded trams and were privileged to see an onsite actual working day at the studio. No shows…No staged performances, an actual working day at a major studio. However, this tour differed from their regular tour.

It was the Sybil Jason tour in that the tour guides explained the various locations where Sybil actually worked. Soundstages were pointed out where Sybil shot certain scenes, the stages where she rehearsed dances with the legendary Busby Berkeley, and especially Stage #17, where Sybil cut the ribbon at the dedication ceremony.

Warner Bros., years ago, had the reputation of being a friendly lot and the fans noticed the same warmth that day which made them feel at ease and comfortable. The tour and the fascinating visit through the Museum took a good three hours and by that time it was time for everyone to go to the Smoke House restaurant right across the street from the studio. Slowly, everyone arrived at the restaurant and after many hugs and kisses and countless photos taken, the group entered a well-appointed private room where Sybil was accompanied by myself, our beautiful daughter Toni and our handsome and bright high-schooler grandson, Daniel. Sybil, between bites of food, was kept busy autographing many items, posing for pictures, and a fan even brought a Sybil Jason doll to the event.

President Gary Heckman addressed the group and acknowledged Vice President Ruth Pollack for her indispensable work putting this special event together. The time passed very quickly and, before we knew it, it was time to get back to the Warner Bros. lot and to the exquisite Ross Theatre.

Sybil and the group passed under the impressive marquee of the Ross Theatre to attend the evening's presentation. Sybil was warmly greeted by the very knowledgeable Museum curator, Leith Adams, and his co-curator, Lisa Janney, who put in a very special effort to make this whole event memorable for Sybil and her fan club members. Sybil posed with large posters they featured from her very first movie for Warners which, much to her amazement, she had never seen before. Later, she was told that they were going to be sent to her home as a gift.

The 500-seat theatre is just a gem, complete with stadium seating, striking curtains and the latest in theatrical lighting, and the projection and sound were the absolute best available. To start the program, Leith Adams took to the stage and gave a brief rundown of the evening's program, which started off with the brilliant Technicolor short in which Sybil starred, *Changing of the Guard*. Both the sound and the print were so beautifully restored that it looked like it may have been shot yesterday!! The highlight of this 19-minute short was a dream sequence where Sybil fronted and danced with the famous Busby Berkeley dancers in a preci-

Warner Bros marque on my dedication day and night on the lot for
my birthday 2005. My fan club members attending.

sion tap routine supposedly in front of Buckingham Palace in London. At
the conclusion, it earned a generous round of applause.

The lights then came up and Leith Adams escorted Sybil to the stage.
He gave some historical highlights about Sybil as the studio's first child star
and then he introduced Sybil, who then took questions from the studio
audience. She was delighted at the questions that Warner personnel put to
her and was relieved to have been able to answer all of them. Later, it was
heard that this was one of the better interviews conducted at the theatre.

After the Q&A session, Mr. Adams escorted Sybil back to her seat,
the lights dimmed, and the main feature, starring Sybil in her first Warner
Bros. movie, *Little Big Shot*, began. The applause at the end was heartwarming and, all of us, thinking that the festivities were over, headed back
up to the lobby, where, much to our surprise, plates of goodies and drinks
were served to everyone.

Sybil glowed with joy when the Warner employees were so generous
in their praises for her work. One gentleman even said, "I wasn't quite
familiar with your work until tonight, but you can bet I am a big fan of
yours now."

After much socializing, the club members and Warner personnel,
everyone en masse, sang a gloriously loud and heartfelt "HAPPY BIRTH-
DAY" to Sybil.

To quote my wife's comment about the event ... "It was an evening I will never forget."

A Treasured One-time Meeting

This is a departure from anything I have ever written before because the subject of your 8x10 I have met only once.

Naturally, I have never worked with him, as he comes from a different era than myself, but I was so very impressed with he and his wife as two beautiful human beings that I thought that you would be interested in my impressions of them both. To give you an idea how and where this meeting took place, the following is what happened in 1992.

Patrick Swayze

In September, Tony and I attended the American Cinema Awards in Beverly Hills and the special event honored Frank Sinatra, Whoopi Goldberg, and Jack Valenti, all of whom attended that night. It took place at the Merv Griffin-owned Beverly Hilton Hotel and as we all arrived individually and the valet took care of our cars, there were trumpeters that blew a tribute to our arrivals. They resembled the trumpeters of ancient times who announced the arrival of British royalty. It made a thrilling arrival for all of us and for the hundreds of fans that were taking pictures that banked both sides of the outside of the building.

I don't believe that this town will ever see such a gathering of stars, both present and past, under one roof, again. Handsome Robert Wagner was master of ceremonies and they did something very unusual that evening. Although the invited audience of 1,200 represented all phases and eras of show business, Bob introduced 300 of us individually to take our bows. What a wonderful "lump in the throat" feeling it was to be bathed in rounds of applause from our peers when we each stood up when our names were called. After a fine dinner, we were treated to a stage show that was not to be believed. Liza Minnelli knocked our socks off with a medley of songs, as did Shirley MacLaine, Betty Garrett (doing numbers that she and Sinatra had done in their movies together), Vanessa Williams, Robert Merrill (of the magnificent voice), and...someone I had not seen since 1936! This gentleman had the energy and the enthusiasm of a young man when he sang and whirled around on stage that night and had the audience in the palm of his hand...It was the great Cab Calloway!! After the show, it was great reminiscing with Cab about *The Singing Kid* and although his memory had a few lapses here and there...who cares??? He was back to being thirty years old that night on stage!

53

There is a very sad ending to this story. Mr. Swayze passed away after a very courageous 20-month battle with cancer on September 14, 2009. However, let us be grateful that he will always be young, virile and stay in our hearts as long as there are his films to enjoy.

Rest in peace, Patrick

About Your 8x10

So many of us attending this wondrous event got to circulate to renew acquaintances and meet some new ones between dinner and after the stage show. As the saying goes, we had "the pick of the litter," with every known celebrity within arms length and all willing to converse. As a matter of fact, it was amusing that before dinner was served those of us sitting at the "kiddie table" (all ex-child stars) got a visit from Tony Curtis, who was a real charmer. He had something to say to each one of us gals, which was very complimentary, and made us all sit up a little straighter and pull in our tummies a wee bit more!!!

As you can imagine, a lot of photos were being taken that evening and it's amazing that most of us didn't get flashbulb "burn," but nobody cared…even some who were known to be divas!! Everyone was willing to pose. As a matter of fact, my dear friend Fayard Nicholas, of the dancing Nicholas Brothers, asked me if I would come with him to a section near the bar to have a picture taken with him and his brother and, of course, I was happy to do so.

While I was gone Tony, my husband, was arranging a surprise for me. He noticed a very handsome man and his lovely wife standing right near where we were stationed at that particular time and asked him if he would be good enough to pose for a picture with me when I returned. Tony had told him that our daughter Toni and I were big fans of his, mentioned who I was, and, bless them, he and his wife graciously waited until I got back. It *was* a wonderful surprise for me for many reasons. I just fell in love with both of them, not as celebrities, but as beautiful human beings. As a couple, they could have been separated by miles of distance yet there was a complete connection of love between them re-gardless of time or space, and for Hollywood that is a miracle that doesn't happen too often between married couples. I think because Tony and I had been married for such a long time and, happily so, we found it easy to recognize this in them. We also appreciated the fact that neither Patrick or

Me and Patrick Swayze at American Cinema Awards.

his wife had assumed the Hollywood tendency called the "wandering eye," which one might assume to mean that a husband or lover makes a visual and flirtatious eye contact with another woman while in the presence of his wife. That is *not* the Hollywood wandering eye. What I'm talking about is when there is an ongoing conversation between two people and when one of them is relating a story, the other person breaks eye contact to look around the room, presumably to see if there is anyone more important than the person he or she is now talking to. Both the Swayzes are very sensitive and classy people; they make you feel that you are the only person in the room and deservedly get their full attention. A very rare attribute in Hollywood.

If you *ever* have the privilege of meeting Patrick and Lisa Swayze, please say a silent prayer for them. In 2008, Patrick was diagnosed with a deadly form of pancreatic cancer, but, at the present time, he is doing remarkably well and hopefully will continue to do so.

[**Note:** Your 8x10 may be a bit blurry, but there was a lot of jostling going on at this event and apparently the photographer got bumped while he was taking our picture. I am sure you won't mind that this photo is far from perfect, but think of it as a memento of a lovely meeting.]

Most people have named *Dirty Dancing* (1987) as their favorite Patrick Swayze movie and although I enjoyed it very much and was mightily impressed with his style of dancing, the movie *Ghost* (1990) continues to be my favorite. I watch it on a regular basis because there is a depth to Swayze that I have never seen before…a beautiful sensitivity and maturity that will hold up for many years to come. If you have never seen *Ghost*, please do.

Dear Members

This newsletter is not typical of the subjects that I usually write about, but, as you read on, you will see that although you would not recognize the subject by sight, just about all of you members will find that he has been part of your lives for many, many years. He certainly was a good part of mine.

Before I get into the in-depth profile of the man who was featured in my fan club's newsletter, I thought it would help to give a generalized background that led up to the relationship between the two of us. I wanted to point out some personal facts and background so that you could get a feel of the man behind his talent and hopefully, the next time you hear one of his songs or a movie that he orchestrated, you will have had more of a personalized view of the man behind the music.

Johnny Green

As long as I can remember, music has always been a part of my life and it all started when I was a baby in my home country of South Africa. On a daily basis our home was always filled with the sound of music either coming from the radio or our phonograph playing records of the popular singers of the day or of my brother, who was studying music, practicing his lessons on the piano. Our mother had a great love for all types of music, from operatic to popular, and, although completely untrained as a musician, she got great pleasure at sitting down at the piano every day and playing songs by ear. My dad loved music, too, but his appreciation ran to pop singers of the day, like Al Jolson. My brother David ultimately became a fine pianist and leader of his own band and ran his school of music in Cape Town for many, many years. My brother was not the only one in our family that was a professional pianist. It was when I was not quite five years old when my sister Anita and I journeyed to London to visit my uncle, my aunt and my grandmother that I met my first world-renown professional singers, composers and entertainers. My uncle was pianist-accompanist to stars like Gracie Fields and Frances Day (a leading chanteuse of that day) and these two ladies became my mentors and encouraged my career as an entertainer and introduced me to the most important of the British entrepreneurs, which led to my start on the British stage.

Frances Day and I made a record for His Masters Voice in 1935 and we were backed up by the famous Mayfair Orchestra headed by Carroll Gibbons. (In 2008 a Frances Day CD was released in London. One of the songs featured was "My Kid's a Crooner," which Frances and I sang and recorded in 1935.) Carroll became a very good friend, as did the man that came after him, Ray Noble, as leader of the Mayfair Orchestra. Ray and Gladys Noble became very close friends, especially when we all lived in California and that friendship extended into many years right up until they decided to retire and return to England.

It's amazing how times sometimes blend into one. In my very first movie for Warner Bros., I sang a song called "Rolling in the Money" and, just two weeks ago, on the Internet, YouTube ran a scene of me singing that song and I understand that in the first two days it received over 40,000 hits. The composers, Mort Dixon and Allie Wrubel, wrote this especially for me and Mort was also the composer of such popular songs as "River, Stay Away from My Door," "Bye, Bye Blackbird," "You're My Everything," "Would You Like to Take a Walk?" and "I Found a Million Dollar Baby (in a Five and Ten Cent Store)."

While in New York, I had the honor of meeting a famous musician-composer and his whole family, which eventually led to a familial association for years to come. But that story will come later as written in the newsletter.

As one can well imagine, doing musicals as Warner Bros. first child star under long-term contract allowed me to associate and work with some of the best musician-composers of all time. The most prominent was that of Harold Arlen and E.Y. "Yip" Harburg, who provided the words and music for the song that Al Jolson and I sung in our movie *The Singing Kid*. When we shot the scene on location, both geniuses came to visit us to see how we were handling their song, "You're the Cure for What Ails Me," and Harold took some home movies of all of us in addition to the ones my guardians took. Harold and "Yip" were both fun-loving men and it was obvious that they loved watching artists sing their songs. Three years after composing songs for *The Singing Kid*, they went on to compose all of the songs for *The Wizard of Oz* and were responsible for giving my friend Judy Garland her signature song, "Over the Rainbow."

Of course, on the Warners lot, there were the geniuses of Max Steiner, Dimitri Tiomkin, and the cream of the crop, Erich Wolfgang Korngold, as well as conductor Leo F. Forbstein. I know I have left out many names, but this is just to give you an idea how very lucky I was to be in the company and to work with some of these people.

And talking about luck…in my social life I had the great honor, more times than just once, of sitting on the piano bench in this musician's home in Hollywood and playing the melody of one of his songs while the composer played the bass. I affectionately called and knew him as "Uncle Jerry," but the world knew him as the musical icon Jerome Kern!!! Later on, my sister Anita and I used to visit his daughter Betty at her apartment in Beverly Hills and we always knew when we sat down to dinner that the soup would be Cream of Mushroom. It never changed, no matter what Betty served as the entree.

I was also very fortunate that when I recorded an album for Decca Records the orchestra that backed me up was the fabulous Victor Young and his orchestra.

I realize this is a very long introduction into my main story of a musician that I loved like a brother, but I felt it would give you an idea how this relationship came about. For business reasons, my guardians and I visited the city of New York many times. On our very first visit, on the recommendation of Carroll Gibbons, as our ship landed from its journey from London to New York in the beginning of 1935, we got in touch with Johnny Green and his family.

From the word *go* the whole family adopted me as one of their own. On a personal note, I got to know the different eras of Greens, which consisted of the grandmother, mother and father of Johnny Green, and that continued into my adulthood. To this day, I have a charm bracelet that the Greens filled up with significant charms and each one was entitled "From Uncle Johnny's grandmother," "From Uncle Johnny's mother and father," and "From Uncle Johnny." As a matter of fact, Johnny Green's mother looked a lot like my own mother and from the very beginning, till the day she died, I called her "Mom Green." I think now is the time that we should get to what I wrote in my newsletter to the members of my fan club.

Johnny Green

Almost into his dotage, John Green was known affectionately by the name of Johnny Green, yet he started out in life in his birth year of 1908 with the impressive name of John Waldo Green. Johnny was always destined for success as he was accepted by Harvard at the tender age of 15 years old and was always proud that he had been a Harvard man!! While in college, the bandleader Guy Lombardo hired him to create dance arrangements for his famous orchestra.

Johnny's love of music was interrupted because his father, although proud of Johnny's "bent" for music, wanted his son to have a more "secure" future and forced him to become a stockbroker. Being a good son, Johnny went along with his dad's wishes, but hated it and quit after six months. He married for the very first time, to a young woman by the name of Carol, and because she encouraged her husband to pursue what he loved the most, it was no coincidence that Johnny composed most of his hit songs that became standards to this day during that marriage. I mentioned at the beginning of this newsletter that I was sure that he be-

The man behind his music, Oscar winner and head of MGM Music Dept., composer Johnny Green and me.

came part of your lives through some of his songs, like "I Cover the Waterfront," "I Wanna Be Loved," "Out of Nowhere," and "Body and Soul." It's possible you danced to them, sang along with the records, and/or left a movie theater or stage production humming some of his catchy tunes.

I could fill a book with some of Johnny's credits, such as being musical director at MGM, leading the orchestra for the Academy Awards seventeen times, receiving Oscar nominations fourteen times and winning five times. You heard his music as arranger, conductor, composer in movies such as *Raintree County, Easter Parade* (he won), *An American in Paris* (he won), *High Society* and *West Side Story* (he won), and, one of my personal favorites, *Oliver!* (he won).

As a matter of fact, when little Mark Lester's voice singing of "Where is Love" turned out to be less than desired, Johnny's daughter Kathe supplied the enchanting voice.

I knew Johnny's second wife quite well, Betty Furness, and it was during this time Johnny would hear me tinkling on the piano. Of course, I only played by ear because I had little time to spare while making movies, but this playing by ear started when I was a mere 15 months old in South Africa. I would listen to songs on the radio and then toddle off to the piano and pick out the melody with one chubby little finger.

I was never nervous playing in front of Johnny because Johnny "was family." By the time I was ten years old and madly in love with all forms of music, I had composed some pop pieces and two concertos. One day Johnny came over to my house and Anita told him about my concertos. He asked me to play them and, of course, I did. Afterwards, Anita asked Johnny if he could recommend a piano teacher for me and he surprisingly told my sister not to give me piano lessons. He explained that learning the intricacies of piano would take away most of my creativity; however, it might be a good idea, later on in my life, if I wanted to pursue music as a profession, to introduce me to a formal education of piano. My mother played by ear, I played by ear, and my daughter Toni also plays by ear. We all could play pop or even classics and if one didn't know that we weren't "legitimate," because we mimicked the real thing so well, they could have been fooled to a certain degree. To be honest, I think Johnny gave the best possible advice because many years later, I tried a few piano lessons, but got so aggravated trying to read the music when it was so easy just to play a piece immediately by ear.

Many years later, when Johnny was very ill, I had composed 14 songs for my musical, *Garage Sale*, and it was possible to get it down in musical form only because I found a marvelous musician that had the patience of Job. As I played the songs, note for note, he would write it down on the sheet music. I sent these songs to Johnny and when he had had the time or energy due to his illness, he went through them and I listened very carefully to his advice on each song over the telephone as he wasn't seeing anyone in person. I had become very friendly and absolutely adored Bunny, his third wife, who was completely devoted to Johnny. As a matter of fact, Bunny had told me that she wished that she had been half as loved as I had been from "Mom Green." However, I told her that she could be proud that she made Johnny's life so much better than it had been in the past.

We all were on the dais of the Al Jolson Society when it was held at the Hollywood Roosevelt Hotel quite a number of years back. As you well know, I had costarred with Jolie and Johnny had arranged some songs for him several times and knew him very well, and Bunny, who was quite a bit younger than Johnny, had been a glamorous leggy showgirl in New York and for a time had gone with Jolie, so we all had our stories about the great Jolson.

One day I received a phone call from Bunny telling me that Johnny had passed away. That hit me like a ton of bricks because, like I said earlier, he was more family than anything else.

Bunny and her family, which consisted of her and Johnny's daughters, Babbie and Kathe, held a beautiful memorial service for Johnny at the Bel-Air Church and the crème de la crème of MGM attended. Icons of the music industry got up and spoke of Johnny's genius and I could see so many stars, like my contemporary Donald O'Connor, nodding in agreement when someone spoke of him as a gentleman and an iconic composer. After the service was over, Donald came up to me and said that he wasn't aware that I was part of the Green family. I told him that by blood I wasn't, but by heart and soul I was and that Bunny had insisted that I sit with the family. Bunny Green was a very caring and classy woman. She tried to invite everyone that had played a part in her husband's life, and that included Betty Furness, his second wife, who was escorted by Cesar Romero.

Whenever Bunny sent me a note or a letter in the past, it always had a cartoon or a picture of a cat on it, so you can imagine how startled I was to receive a letter from her about six months *after* her death. It was at Xmas time and apparently a few weeks before she passed away she wrote this same kind of letter to the people she cared about. She said when she knew that she didn't have too much longer upon this earth she decided to do everything that she had never done before but had wanted to...and she did!

Enclosed was a picture of her taken in front of a private airplane. I have stored her letter in a very safe place so, unfortunately, I cannot recall whether she had taken flying lessons or had just taken a trip on that private plane or a helicopter. It was so like that dear lady to think ahead and plan all of this out and contact her dear friends after she was gone in this unique manner.

This was not the end of my contact with the Green family. Johnny and Bunny's daughters knew how close I was to the family and because their dad was reluctant to tell them too much about family history, they got in touch with me and, of course, I was delighted to tell them as much as I knew about their grandmother, grandfather and their great grandmother.

Both the girls have followed in their father's footsteps and have pursued a musical career in different phases of it.

I hope that everyone who reads this newsletter will take into consideration the story behind the *real* human being when they hear his music from now on. Johnny would have liked that and so would have Bunny.

They Earned Their Angel Wings Here On Earth

We hear a lot about charities headed by stars of today and they are to be congratulated to extend themselves to advance the good for others in need. Not to take anything away from them at all, but show-biz people have been doing this type of work for a very long time.

I remember my dear friend, Mr. Joe Weber, of the famous vaudeville team of Weber and Fields, saying that in his memory charity went back to his co-worker's day, the famous Lillian Russell. He said that when "one of our own" got into financial trouble, without fail, the hat would be passed around until the crisis had been solved.

I remember spending the evening, along with my sister Anita and my uncle, at George Burns and Gracie Allen's home with Jack Benny and his wife and two other couples in attendance. They got to talking about their days in vaudeville and when they got to the subject of passing the hat around, Mr. Benny reminded Mr. Burns that he had been a recipient of that generosity many times himself. Through the smoke of his ever-present cigar, George good-naturedly nodded his head in agreement.

Everyone was reminiscing about the good old days and how George Burns and Jack Benny were always the first celebrities to volunteer their time to worthwhile charities. I was very privileged to be one of many guest stars at a charity that was headed by Jack Benny and Dick Powell that was held at the Shrine Auditorium in January 1936 to raise funds for Mount Sinai Home. To name just a few of the guest stars at that benefit, there were Charlotte Greenwood (the lady with the long legs who danced in many 20th Century-Fox movies), Mickey Rooney, Bela Lugosi, James Dunn, and singer-comedian Pinky Tomlin.

Another benefit, held at The Carthay Circle Theatre, on January 16, 1936, was to aid the 200 tubercular patients at Duarte Sanatorium and also the maternity and Clinic Wards at Cedars Lebanon Hospital. That show was also led by Jack Benny and attended by many, including Allan Jones (who many years later sang one of my songs that I wrote for my musical *Garage Sale*), Dick Foran (who did such a fine job as the countrified boyfriend of Bette Davis in *The Petrified Forest*), and so many others. It would take a book to name the charities that I did, starting with my baby appearances in South Africa, in Canada, all over the United States and the ones I still do up to this present day. It's my pleasure to attend these benefits because that's exactly what they do…they benefit people who need a boost up what happens to everyone some time in their lives.

Talking from personal experience, I was only three or four years old when I did my first charity performance in South Africa. I belonged to a dance class where all of us kids learned routines and then performed them for different organizations as part of a fundraiser. When I was not quite five years old and just about ready to leave South Africa for London, I had become a star attraction as a solo act and did one last performance which was attended this time by British royalty. I was doing my usual act, starting off in the earliest part of the evening with my imitations of famous stars and later ending with a very popular song, at that time, called "Lily of Laguna." The stage was dark except for a spotlight on me as I sang my final song. However, it puzzled me that in the middle of that song I heard a rumble of laughter coming from the audience. My sister always told me that if I was dancing and perhaps part of my costume fell off, I was just to ignore it and go on with my act as if nothing had happened. That night, when the show was over and I asked why people were laughing when I sang my song, I got a gentle lesson on show-business etiquette from my sister Anita. She explained the reason for the laughter while I was singing that lovely sentimental song "Lily of Laguna." We had never went into

Benefit for a paraplegic young girl. Me in a Becky hat holding a blowup of Shirley Temple and I from *The Little Princess* which brought a big amount at auction.

Auction gathering to benefit Tippi Hendren's Animal Sanctuary.
(*back row left to right*) Mrs. Fayard Nicholas, Delmar Watson, Alan Seuss, Unknown, Earl Holliman, Ann Jeffries, Marsha Hunt. (*second row left to right*) Jane Kean, Giselle Mackenzie, Margaret O'brien, Unknown, Fayard Nicholas, Tippi Hedren,Eric Madden (Highest bidder of the evening) Sybil Jason.
(*sitting left to right*) Unknown, Unknown, Terry Moore, a Chaplin mimic.

specifics in regards to the ruling that no matter what happens during one's act, one must just ignore it uninterrupted. Well, as a good performer, I *didn't* interrupt my song. On the other hand (both literally and figuratively), I also did not ignore the itch that started in a *very* private place, but satisfied the urge to scratch it mid-song. An audience, including royalty, is very forgiving when one is only five years old!

I did several charity performances in London, which I have explained in my previous books led to appearances in two British movies, stage appearances in various parts of England and finally earning me a contract to Warner Bros. which brought me over to America. Then and now, some of these charities were for small groups and others were for amazingly large presentations with a list of the greatest icons in show business appearing in support of the charity. Many years later, when I was an adult, it was interesting when quite frequently someone would approach me and tell me that they were present in past years when I was making an appearance for a worthwhile cause. One evening, in the 1980s, I was a guest star at a women's show-business club function, which was going to give the proceeds of that evening to a well-known charity. I did a monologue set to the music of *The Way We Were* with appropriate but changed words to fit the subject matter of that evening.

Later on, after I had done my act, a lady came up to me and said that when I was just a little girl she remembered me being partially responsible for raising enough money to rebuild a rectory of the church that she belonged to in New York. I believe she said it was a church right near where John Lennon had been assassinated. To be very honest about this, I didn't remember that particular one only because I did a lot of charities when I was on tour. One that does come to mind that I *do* remember is when I was given a beautiful gold Los Angeles police badge done in miniature form because I had raised a great amount of money to build the training division for police officers at Elysian Park in our City of Angels. To go along with the badge, I was also made honorary Captain of the Los Angeles police just before I boarded a float in the Rose Parade. You can imagine how excited I was being such a young child to receive such an honor.

Stories of this nature continually turn up. Not ten years ago a South African reporter in Johannesburg did a feature article on me that updated

At Tippi Hedren's auction. Margaret O'Brien, Delmar Watson, and me.

the people of my birth country about my present activities and alerted them that I had an international fan club, but so far there were no South African members. It was not long before quite a few did join the fan club, but there was one letter that the new member included with her sign-up which stood out in my memory and really touched me greatly. It was from a lady who, in 1941, was a child living in an orphanage in Johannesburg.

At that time, I was doing a personal appearance tour throughout South Africa and was pretty near preparing to return to America and my contract at Fox studios, but, of course, that never happened because of the attack on Pearl Harbor. My family did not want me traveling in wartime and, rather than repeat another separation of years to come after I returned to America, they preferred that I stay with the family in South Africa. However, before the dreadful news of the attack on Pearl Harbor was known, this South African lady said that she and all of her fellow orphans in 1941 were told to put on their Sunday best and gather on the school playground because a real movie star from Hollywood was going to visit with them. She told me that she was very nervous just before my arrival because although we were all approximately the same age, she didn't know how I would react toward them. In her letter she said that she never forgot how I *did* treat them for they were made to feel like I was one of them and they talked about that visit of mine for years to come. That certainly was a letter I have always treasured.

Not too long ago, a Canadian member of my fan club, by the name of Midge Reese, sent me a copy of a newspaper clipping about when I visited a children's hospital in Ontario in 1937 while I was on tour throughout the USA and Canada. This appearance I *do* remember quite clearly because, although I was only about eight years old, I was emotionally affected by seeing such young children in all stages of pain due to diseases or trying to recuperate after serious operations. I performed for them, spoke to each one of them and in the interim realized how very lucky I was to be so healthy.

I could go on and on giving you examples of what so many of us did in between acting in movies during the Golden Era, but I think that you now realize that charity went way further back than the '30s and '40s and continues on to this day. Please, let me take my hat off to Elizabeth Taylor, who took on the humongous job of trying to raise funds to help research find a cure for the horrid disease of AIDS. When

Taken at auction and benefit for Variety Arts in Beverly Hills
Me and Mr. Blackwell, the designer.

she first started, she basically stood alone in her efforts to get funding because this was a very unpopular cause. But she stuck with it and thanks to her persistence and big heart many millions have been raised for research to stem and hopefully eradicate this disease that has spread worldwide.

The same goes for Danny Thomas, who founded the St. Jude charity, who magnanimously announces that no child will ever be sent away from treatment because of lack of funds. In this present day and age, Angelina Jolie and Brad Pitt have done wonders for their various charities and they are to be commended, especially when the economy has hit so hard at the many charitable organizations that have been running out of funds because the general public are less willing or unable to finance them with donations.

I don't think I have ever refused to make an appearance to benefit someone worse off than myself. It usually turns out to be a happy and fulfilling experience for me. In the 1980s an industrialist and his wife who lived two or three doors away from our home in Studio City asked me if I would make an appearance at their estate for a group of Mexican-American orphans that they sponsored yearly. Many of these kids had been in trouble in various ways, but I am sure a lot of it was as a result of unfortunate circumstances due to lack of love or loss of parents either by death or by desertion. Some of them were hard cases and at first no matter what I said or did I didn't seem to be getting through to them. Then the subject of school came up and I got to telling them the difficulties of trying to get three hours of work in on a daily basis while working on a movie. They seemed quite interested that I still had to keep up in school even though I was a "movie star." One of the kids asked me if my mother or father ever helped me with my homework and that became the ice breaker. They related when I told them that I hadn't seen my family at that time in almost eight years because I came from a different country and my parents couldn't leave South Africa because they had to tend to my other siblings. They somehow related to me being "without parents." We bonded from then on and I felt especially close to one of the older girls who never said much. I was told that she was continually in trouble with the law and was listed as incorrigible. I honestly didn't see a hardness in her. I saw vulnerability, perhaps a bit of paranoia, but deep down I think she wanted what we all want in life…to be loved and appreciated. I asked her if she would write to me every now and again and at first she was reluctant. She asked me why I would want to hear from her and I told her that I liked her and had a feeling that she would do well in life once she decided what career she wanted to follow. I didn't hear from her for several weeks, but one day I received a very short note from her and she told me that she had decided to do better in school and that she had just gotten a part-time job as a babysitter. After that, I thought I would hear from her on a regular basis, but that was not the case. In fact, I didn't hear from her for over two years and I came to the realization that continuing on a correspondence with me was not one of her priorities. I felt sad, but knew that the worst thing I could do was to push a connection that she wasn't interested in.

Three years had gone by before one day, in amongst my mail, I saw an envelope with a very official seal on it and a return address that I was not familiar with. As I opened up the envelope, I saw that it was an invitation and as I read further, tears started to well up in my eyes. It was my Mexican-American orphan who had turned her whole life around and had worked hard and studied to become a member of the Los Angeles Police force and this was an invitation to her graduation. I cannot tell you the pride I felt for this young woman at the ceremony. She had lost a great deal of weight and had gained a great deal of self-confidence and was now in a relationship with a very nice young man who was also in the police force. The very last time that I heard from her, she was still with the department, was now happily married and was expecting a baby. I went to the christening and only found out at the ceremony that they had named their baby daughter…Sybil!

I have also had some funny experiences connected with appearing for charities. My husband, Tony, and I had a very good friend that dated back to when she was only 16 years old and we were in the early stages of dating. We kept up the friendship with Shirley Mason and were delighted when she announced that she and her boyfriend, Ralph Fierro, were getting married. As time went along, both she and Ralph were heavily into sponsoring Mexican-American kids that needed a helping hand. The Fierros had a lovely large home in Glendale and one day they asked me if I would appear as a guest star and show some of my movies for those who would attend a gathering at their home. Of course, the answer was yes and the evening was a great success, I am happy to report. Shirley and Ralph had the unique idea to supply a goodly amount of beans to stock the pantry of the Home that these kids were staying at and the entrance fee to seeing my presentation was a minimum of two pounds or more of sacks of beans to attend the "show." There is an old show-business expression that goes way back in time so you can just imagine what a real charge I got out of literally and figuratively "working for beans" that evening!! It was a delightful experience and a good time was had by all!!

Frieda Inescort

One of the first actresses that I featured for the members of the Sybil Jason International Fan Club was the Scottish-born actress Frieda Inescort. I was fortunate to have portrayed her daughter twice in movies that were produced by Warner Brothers and later at Republic. This is what I wrote in the newsletter.

About Your 8x10

I thought perhaps you'd like to hear a story about your most recent autographed picture and the lady in it with me. I'm sure most people fondly remember Frieda Inescort as portraying the elegant lady in many movies and to mention just one, as the mother of Elizabeth Taylor in the classic *A Place in the Sun*. I was very fortunate to have had her portray my mother in two movies and you will be pleased to know that Miss Inescort was as elegant and very much the lady off screen as she was on screen.

The photo that you now have came from the 1937 Warner Bros. movie *The Great O'Malley*, and was directed by a gentleman by the name of William Dieterle. Mr. Dieterle was undoubtedly one of Hollywood's most brilliant directors, but he earned a rightful reputation of being impatient and lacking gentleness of manner with his actors. I only mention this because it will help to illustrate that not only was Miss Inescort a dedicated actress, she was also a very brave lady.

In the movie, I was her crippled daughter and as such she was required to pick me up in her arms and carry me into another room and gently put me on a couch. This was no easy task for, besides my own body weight, I was wearing a five-pound steel brace on my leg (to keep it straight) under my black stockings. The first time that we did the scene, Miss

71

The Great O'Malley, 1937. Me and Frieda Inescourt.

Inescort's arms seem to give way and she dropped me unharmed onto the couch. The director loudly chided her for being so clumsy, but, being the lady that she was, she apologized and said she would try and do better. The next time the shot was perfect!! What nobody knew was that for many years she was suffering from the debilitating and progressive muscle disease of multiple sclerosis.

I have just repeated a version of what I wrote in my first book, *My Fifteen Minutes*, in my Humphrey Bogart chapter. The following was not in my newsletter, but I felt it needed expanding for a specific reason. Taking into consideration of how Miss Inescort, who was emotionally and, at times, physically abandoned when she was a child, only a psychologist could explain how, as an adult, she put up so graciously with the unfeeling remarks aimed at her by our director on that set. Some of the information in the following came from various articles that I read about Miss Inescort, but also because of the many conversations that she and my sister Anita had in between scenes on *The Great O'Malley*, I can validate most of the following, intentionally leaving out any information I did not hear for myself.

Frieda's parents met when her father, journalist Jock Wrightman a Scotsman, came to review a play that her mother was in and after a very short courtship they married in 1899. Frieda was born in Edinburgh, Scotland, but when she was just a baby of three years old, her mother, Elaine, who was a very ambitious woman, left Scotland to go to her native country England to further her stage career. She took Frieda with her, but, finding that a small child just got in the way of her progress as an actress, she left little Frieda with a family in Surrey, England. Not two years later, Frieda was once again uprooted to live with another family in Rhyl, Wales. Miss Inescort told Anita that this was one of the unhappiest times of her young life as she always remembered being cold because of the damp climate and not being near her mother. Her mother was now legally separated from her father and then made another decision that changed the sweet nature of her daughter Frieda to a rebellious and uncontrollable child when she was once again moved to a boarding school in Essex. Ultimately, she was expelled for misconduct; however, her spirits lifted when in 1910 there was a reconciliation between her parents and they once again became a family and situated in London. This, unfortunately, did not last long because Frieda was once again sent to another school and in 1911 her father, in frustration, finally divorced her mother because she had had an adulterous affair. Once again, Frieda's ever-changing world was uprooted when she accompanied her mother and her mother's lover on a ship sailing to New York to further Elaine Inescourt's stage career. That never happened because she wasn't able to obtain any parts on Broadway and had to settle for signing a contract with a touring company, which was a big step down in her determination to become a star on the Broadway stage. Frieda was ultimately boarded at Holy Rosary School in Long Island but when Elaine Inescort's lover abandoned them and her tour ended, she and Frieda returned to London and her young daughter was once again sent away to a convent school.

Frieda, at the vulnerable young age of sixteen, graduated from the convent school in London, but, when she joined her mother in London, she was in for yet another emotional shock. She was told that she must make her own way in life and, to add insult to injury, her mother, in social situations, passed Frieda off as her sister.

Frieda Inescort started out her "adult" life by obtaining many non-theatrical jobs and supporting herself. However, one night, while attending a Broadway play, she went backstage to see Molly Pearson, whom she had known when she was a youngster. When she asked Ms. Pearson why the lead character in the play had been played by an American when it was usually always portrayed by a British girl, she was told that English girls were hard to find at that time in New York and suggested that Frieda pursue an acting career herself. Frieda had never considered becoming an actress, but for some strange reason decided to write a letter to a producer whom she had met in England. Ultimately, he gave her a small part in his next play when she read for him and impressed him enough to take a chance on her.

She did, however, keep her day job, realizing, through her mother's bad experiences, how unpredictable show business could be. Ironically the play she was in was such an enormous success that in time she had to give up her nine-to-five job to be able to accept more prestigious offers on stage. But, in the interim, and before she left that job, she had met a gentleman by the name of Ben Ray Redman who worked at the same place as Frieda. They fell in love and married in 1926. By this time, her mother Elaine was so resentful of Frieda's success on stage, realizing that she had never attained anything near what her daughter was achieving. In retaliation, she absolutely refused to talk to Frieda. Miss Inescort told Anita how much she was hurt by, once again, being abandoned emotionally by her mother, which was just another dart aimed at her wellbeing. In

Frieda, me, and Henry Wilcoxen from *Woman Dr.*, 1938.

spite of this, it seemed that, at long last, Frieda Inescort's life was approaching some semblance of normalcy and success.

Frieda had never considered a Hollywood career, even though she had been offered the opportunity several times, but when her husband was offered a very lucrative job at Universal Studios in Hollywood as a literary adviser they soon packed up and relocated to California. Not the type of woman to just sit around the house when her husband was at work, almost immediately on arrival she took a part in a stage play at a Los Angeles theatre and very quickly, because some talent scouts saw her in the play and was impressed with her performance, she was signed to a contract with Samuel Goldwyn Productions.

I don't think I need to expound on her career in Hollywood because that is so well known, but, regardless, her continuing career was not all peaches and cream. Later, when she was signed to a Warner Bros. contract, she soon realized that the real reason she had been signed was to keep the studio's leading female star, Kay Francis, in line.

By the way, this was not an unusual practice, but was used at most of the studios at that time. As an example, years later, Kim Novak was signed to Columbia to keep Rita Hayworth in line. Warners found that Frieda's type of elegance was hard to use, so they loaned her out to other studios and two of her better roles that she was highly praised for was as a lawyer in *Portia on Trial* (1937) and for her leading role in *Woman Doctor* (1939), both at Republic. When we were making *Woman Doctor*, she told Anita that she and her husband were getting more and more disenchanted with Hollywood and apparently that was no exaggeration because in 1944 they pulled up stakes and moved back to New York. Frieda went back to her roots on the stage and was highly praised for all her appearances. In late 1948, she returned to Hollywood to appear in a movie where she could display her acting chops at long last in the movie *The Judge Steps Out* and, then, in 1950, to dip her toes experimentally in the water and venture toward her television debut in the *Fireside Theater* series on NBC.

The next ten years were fairly busy, but in 1960 she often felt dizzy and extremely disoriented. Very concerned, she consulted her doctor, who finally diagnosed her with multiple sclerosis. Her doctors in the 1930s had suspected she *might* have a muscular disease; this was before the term multiple sclerosis became the word for it. Because she was stumbling and using a cane by 1961, she decided to retire rather than hold up expensive productions with her disability. One always hopes for a happy ending for courageous and generous people, but 1961 was probably one of the worst for Frieda Inescort. Her husband, Ben, had been despondent for a long time. After a meal at a restaurant, he returned home and went upstairs to bed. I never found out where Miss Inescort was at that time, but apparently she didn't accompany him home because he called her and told her he had taken some pills because he was extremely depressed on the state of the world and couldn't face up to it any longer. She immediately called an ambulance, but, by the time the paramedics arrived, Ben Ray Redman was dead.

That apparently had shocked Frieda's system because her disease from then on accelerated. It did not help that in 1964 she heard that her mother had died at the age of 87.

I will always admire Frieda Inescort's courage and her unflinching will to go on. She worked for the Multiple Sclerosis Society and in her wheelchair often collected donations for them in various parts of the city.

Frieda died at 5:00 p.m. on February 26, 1976, at the Country Home Hospital in Woodland Hills, California, and according to her wishes was cremated at the Rosedale Cemetery.

The following is more of what I wrote in my newsletter to the members of my fan club.

In 1939, after I had left Warner Bros. and before I was signed by 20th Century-Fox, I made one of the first non-Western movies at Republic, *Woman Doctor*. There were two other Warner Bros. alumnus in that movie and it was like old home week. It starred Frieda Inescort, who portrayed my mother once again, and the actress that was the *femme fatale* in the movie *The Singing Kid*, and was once again the *femme fatale*, Claire Dodd. Cast as my father was an actor by the name of Henry Wilcoxon, who had starred in many movies, including playing Antony in *Cleopatra* with Claudette Colbert. Ultimately, Henry became Cecil B. DeMille's right-hand man at Paramount, but, in 1939, I became very friendly with Henry and his lovely actress wife, Joan Woodbury, and was often invited to their home and magnificent ranch for fun weekends. Incongruously, even though I had no scenes with Claire Dodd in *The Singing Kid*, off the set of *Woman Doctor*, she, Henry, and my sister Anita and I hung out together almost every day at lunchtime at a favorite restaurant right near the studio, but strangely enough that did not include Frieda. Not that we wouldn't have loved to have had her, but she was a very private lady and retired to her dressing room at lunchtime. I smile when I remember what a good sense of humor she had when Henry Wilcoxon used to call her Frieda Inter-course!! She was not as straight-laced as some of the roles she depicted, and I think secretly she got a real charge out of Henry's nickname for her. I wish that her life had been more enjoyable because she gave so much of herself in the movies she appeared in and, sadly, she really deserved better than she ever got!!

Beverly Roberts

Unlike the personalities I have featured in my other two books, it is to this very day a puzzlement that I have scant on set memories of Beverly Roberts. I am just guessing at this but I presume that it may have been because her very first movie was as Al Jolson's romantic interest in our 1936 movie, *The Singing Kid*, and she may have been quite nervous appearing with such an icon at a comparatively young age and took the opportunity in between scenes for some down time to herself. I have some marvelous home movies taken on location that showed a lot of our fun activities as well as some of our rehearsal times that were shot by my guardian as well as the home movies that the composer of our songs for that movie, Harold Arlen, took of all of us…but Beverly was missing in both home movies.

What I *do* remember is that Beverly had a warm and cheerful personality and an extremely sexy Margaret Sullavan-type voice and laugh. I do have a faint memory that, sometimes, on the sidelines, Beverly would sit quietly and talk to my sister Anita or to the dialogue girl, but, other than that, I don't even recall her at lunchtime when stars and crew alike would gather around the location truck for our catered lunchboxes. How things have changed in this day and age when the meals provided for stars and crew could be classified as four-star gourmet meals. Most of our location meals in the thirties consisted of a sandwich, maybe a piece of chicken, potato salad, an apple and cookies. The only hot thing served was off a truck that always had hot coffee, hot chocolate or tea at the ready. As you can see, no one was ever really "catered to," meal-wise, but seeing that there never were any complaints it stayed par for the course for many years.

It's hard to believe, but, on May 19, 2009, my dear friend Beverly Roberts turned 92 years old and still bends down and touches her toes with ease. On her birthday, I phoned her at home and was most amused that one of her *very* few complaints in Life is that just recently the Department of Motor Vehicles took away her driver's license, quoting Beverly, "*Not* because I wasn't physically capable of driving a car, but simply because of my age!!" I am in awe of her and although I do not have vivid memories of her in between the scenes of *The Singing Kid* (this lapse is *very* unusual for me), for a number of wonderful years in recent times we have had great times and have done quite a few personal appearances together when *The Singing Kid* is shown at various venues. We have also met socially when my husband Tony was still alive and we drove down to her home in Laguna in California. Nowadays, our daughter Toni has taken over for her dad and when we drive down to Laguna she, too, finds Beverly a lot of fun. One thing I will always cherish is her kindness and warmth of heart when she regularly checked on me via telephone (it's quite a trek from L.A. to Laguna) after my husband passed away in July of 2005. When one considers that Beverly and I did not have a social relationship until a number of years ago, her concern with my wellbeing at that sad time sometimes overshadowed close friends of mine of many years.

It's been countless years since I have been named as an honorary lifetime member of the Al Jolson Society and have appeared at many venues around the United States for them. However, I couldn't understand why (because so very few of us who had worked with that world-famous icon are still alive) the Society never asked Beverly to be a guest star at their banquets, even though I had suggested this many times and provided them with her phone number and address. Finally, a very talented entertainer who was a board member of the Society and had become a very good friend of mine, Richard Halpern, saw to it that Beverly was invited to the great banquet they held at the famous Hollywood Roosevelt Hotel in Hollywood. Ultimately, and with no surprise to me, the members and guests who attended this gathering were thrilled to meet her and she looked wonderful and was full of vitality and the fans had a multitude of questions to ask her. I was so pleased with her popularity. It was not long after that banquet that we jointly attended quite a number of venues that started featuring the showing of *The Singing Kid*. However, you must remember that Beverly had quite a movie career *after* doing this movie, which just happened to be her very first appearance on the screen.

Years ago, after I was an adult, it was truly a red-letter day for me when I first heard about Beverly from one of the members of the Jolson

Main picture of me and Beverly from *The Singing Kid*, 1936.
(*Inset*) Late 1990's at a showing of *The Singing Kid*.

Society that was visiting New York from Ohio. Beverly, at that time in 1954, lived in New York and had been appointed administrator for Theatre Authority that had jurisdiction over members appearing at charity functions and telethons. In the midst of the Ohio man catching up with Beverly's past movie career, my name came up and Beverly was delighted to hear that I was living in California and was now (gasp) a married lady. Naturally, as soon as I received her address and phone number, I wrote her a letter and gave her an update of myself and my family and mentioned that I hoped one day we could once again meet. I found out that after *The Singing Kid* she starred opposite Humphrey Bogart in *Two Against the World* and, generally considered her biggest film, *God's Country and the Woman,* co-starring with George Brent. This movie was first offered to none other than Bette Davis, but she turned it down, and they handed the woman's lead over to Beverly! I believe in the late '40s and early '50s she had several radio and television appearances, but she always preferred doing stage work. With that wonderful voice of hers, I can see why stage was a great venue for her. In 1977, Beverly decided to retire to that lovely community in California called Laguna Niguel and has been enjoying her life to the extreme since then.

A few years back, the prestigious Southern California University of UCLA held a special Sybil Jason evening at their famous theatre complex and part of the program was a showing of *The Singing Kid* and my Technicolor short called *Changing of the Guard*, which featured me and the Buz Berkeley girl dancers in a dream sequence where the girls backed me up in a precision tap dance. A week before my special evening, I gave some needed information to the man who was going to present me to the audience that night and when we got to the subject of *The Singing Kid*, I mentioned that Beverly and I were the only survivors of that movie. My interviewer's eyes lit up and he asked if I would mind if they invited Beverly to attend. With matching enthusiasm, I told him where he could contact her; I told him, by all means, I would be delighted for them to invite her to sit with me at the Q&A session after *The Singing Kid* showing. What an evening that was and Beverly and I had a ball sitting together reminiscing about that movie.

As an actress, and certainly as a woman, Beverly Roberts is an inspiration with her youthful and optimistic outlook on Life. I can assure you that I am most fortunate to be able to call her Friend...A friend that is 92 years old, going on twenty, who enjoys life 7/24.

All Work and No Glory

This chapter, I think, is going to be quite unique in that I don't believe that anyone has ever covered this subject to any great degree before in a show-business book. I am hoping that you find it both interesting and informative.

To start with, since most of my readers are movie buffs, they are quite familiar with the profession of the stand-in. However, I made several inquiries before I decided to do this chapter and found out that, generally, most people are unaware how extensive and hard the duties of the men, women and—yes, children—are who work sometimes on a regular basis as stand-ins. Because of their efforts, they make life so much easier for the stars of the movie. When the movie audience sees a very intimate and dramatic scene in a movie, they do not realize that the actor doing that scene is surrounded by many people. These people are indispensable to a production and are experts in their individual field and are needed onsite.

During the day-to-day production of a movie, an actor is faced with the presence of the director, cinematographer, the assistant director, the dialogue girl, the head gaffer (the man in charge of the men manning the lights on the immediate set and also from a catwalk above the set), the prop men, the still photographers, the sound man that monitors each and every scene for clarity of sound, the boom man (responsible for the microphone that usually dangles above the head of the actor and out of camera range), the "extras," the wardrobe and makeup people and…The Stand In. So much for the intimacy that an actor strives for in a scene where so many eyes are a witness to their emotions.

One of the signs that an actor knows that he "has arrived" is when he is given his own stand-in. Not everyone is fortunate enough to have one and this is usually determined by the amount of scenes you have in a production.

It is no secret that an inordinate amount of time is spent "setting up the lights" and camera angles, repositioning the actors' "marks," if necessary (usually pieces of tape stuck to the floor and out of camera range), and a multitude of other things that may pop up with regularity much to the frustration of the director and cinematographer. Without exaggeration, any of these problems could take up to a full hour at a time. Can you imagine what the actor would look and feel like having to stand so long under those hot lights? Things nowadays have improved considerably since the thirties and forties because the intensity of the lights is not required to be as hot, something which used to become almost unbearable. That was usually the state we were in especially when shooting in Technicolor because the heat was double that of the black-and-white lighting. Naturally, we could not get relief through air conditioning because the sound man would have picked the noise up. Enter the stand-in.

I was one of the fortunate ones from the very beginning with my first movie for Warner Bros., *The Little Big Shot*, to be immediately assigned a stand in. More about that later. I like to think of the first day on a movie set as a roundtable conference. It's a combination of the initial meeting between the stars and their director to discuss the overall storyline of the whole scenario and then specifically what would be shot that day. Sometimes there is even a run-through of the dialogue, but that decision is usually left up to the director. Some do not believe in too much preparation because they feel that it takes away the spontaneity and freshness from the actor. On the other hand, others swear by the blow-for-blow preparation.

On our very first day, Robert Armstrong, Edward Everett Horton, Glenda Farrell and myself sat at the table listening to what director Michael Curtiz expected from us and what he wanted to accomplish overall. I have to tell you that at no point in time did I feel that I was talked down to simply because I was a child. In everyone's eyes I was a fellow actor and thankfully that was par for the course throughout my acting career.

When our roundtable conference dispersed and we were told to take some time out while our director and cinematographer consulted on some technical things, my sister and I then became acquainted with my very own "on the set" school teacher, Ms. Lois Horn. Lois was a no-nonsense kind of teacher and barring a certain kind of gruffness of manner, she was, in essence, an extremely kind and caring human being and became a close and special friend to my sister Anita and myself.

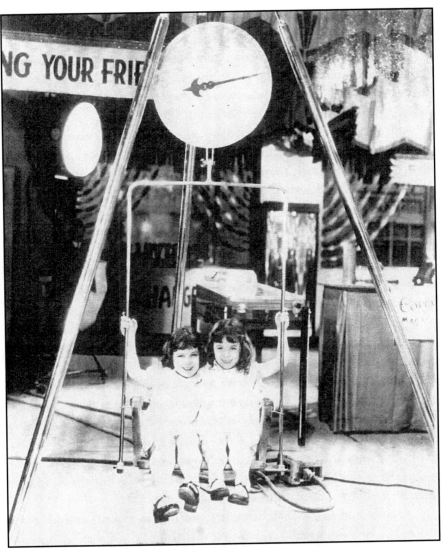

Me and my stand-in Dorothy Brent taken on the set of *Little Big Shot*, 1935.

As I looked around the set where everyone was busily engaged in their various duties in preparation for our first scene to be shot, I noticed a little girl approximately my age standing quietly on the sidelines. At first I thought that maybe she was a visitor and belonged to someone working on our movie, but when I mentioned this to Miss Horn she explained that the little girl would be my stand-in. I had never heard that expression before. Although I did two movies in England, the smallness of my parts did not require a stand-in. After Lois explained what the duties of that little girl would be, she excused herself and brought the little girl over to where our "on-set classroom" would be and did the introductions.

Dorothy Brent and I immediately bonded. Although I had always been more comfortable in the company of adults, it was very easy to like this sweet-natured little girl who, after all, was in the same profession as I was and was also quite comfortable in the adult world.

All during the production of *The Little Big Shot*, Lois tutored both of us in our school lessons. After that, on other Warner Bros. productions that I worked on, much to our disappointment, Dorothy was tutored by another teacher and Lois Horn was strictly assigned to me. Although it was a big disappointment, it did make sense. When I was away from the camera and doing my school work, it was then that Dorothy would stand in my place under the hot lights and move as instructed by the director and cinematographer toward the various floor marks where I would be stationed in the course of the scene. Many times this could take up to an hour while the lights are being adjusted, props rearranged, carpentry noises going on, light measures being taken at each position. This latter job is done by placing a small device that is held up to the face to measure the intensity of the lights and give a reading of same.

Stand-ins don't necessarily have to look *exactly* like you, but should be the same height, have the same complexion, and the same hair color as yours. Dorothy differed slightly in some ways, but they didn't count in the long run for her duties as my stand-in. She had brown eyes as opposed to my blue ones and her hair was dark brown and much longer than mine and curly, as opposed to my straight Dutch boy bob, but those, technically, were minor considerations.

One would think that being a stand-in was a peaches-and-cream profession, but you have to realize that without air conditioning, adult or child could and did swelter for any amount of time spent under those hot lights.

Some stars never develop a relationship with their stand-ins outside of the studio walls, but there are exceptions to that rule. The one I am most familiar with are Errol Flynn's buddies who he socialized with on and off the set. As a matter of fact, it was a rare sight not to see Errol's stand-in, Jim Fleming, and his stuntman, Buster Wiles, by his side while out on the town in the evenings.

Many, many years later, my husband Tony and I became very friendly with Dean Martin's and George Raft's stand-ins. They were part of our beach group on weekends and the most prevalent remarks we heard from them was how loyal and generous these stars were to them.

I am often asked what the difference is between a stand-in and a double. My answer would be, like night and day. In a minimal sort of way I have just explained the basics of what the stand-in does, but, to be honest with you, I wouldn't want any of my loved ones to be a double because it is a very dangerous profession.

For obvious reasons, a double should look as much like the star as physically possible. However, in a lot of cases, predicated on the individual expertise of the double and the stunts that they were required to do, a woman would double for a male star and vice versa. As I mentioned earlier, a gentleman, who happened to be a midget, even doubled for me dressed in a duplicate of my dress, a wig like my Dutch boy bob, my coat, my shoes, and my little boater hat. Fortunately, it was not a dangerous stunt so my memory of it was not at all disturbing.

However, on the same movie, *The Captain's Kid*, all of us (the main stars) went on location to San Pedro in California and one young woman in her very early twenties joined us. Anita and I became very friendly with her because she had a great sense of humor and kept both of us laughing about her experiences as a stuntwoman. She was not going to do any work on our movie, but hitched the ride because the movie she was assigned to was also located in San Pedro.

As we arrived at our destination, our young friend said that if her scheduled work on the other movie went smoothly and took just a short while to do, she would join us on the way back to the studio later on. By late afternoon, after our cameraman said that the sun was no longer good for the "shoot," we prepared to start our journey back to the studio. Because our young stunt lady had not joined us, we assumed that there was a delay in her work on the movie, which often happened, and she would get another ride back with her immediate movie crew. Once we got back to the studio, we noticed a gathering of a few people who joined some of our crew getting off our ride. The news was shattering. Something went very wrong at that other movie location and that lovely young stuntwoman had been killed doing what essentially was not that dangerous. It was just a matter of bad timing between the car she was driving and another one which was supposed to barely miss hitting her. It *did* hit her and although the people in the other car came out of it all right, she was killed instantly. Her fate may have been written on the wind, so to speak, because Tony and I knew a gentleman that was a legend at the stuntmen organization who had been a double since he was in his early thirties and he was still working regularly at the age of seventy years old with not a scratch visible. Everyone from stars down to his cohorts knew Wally Rose.

Also during my adult years I became acquainted with Bette Davis's stand-in who at that time had a little secondhand shop in West Hollywood just off Santa Monica Boulevard. When I used to visit her, she had me laughing and in stitches with the stories she told of her years with Ms. Davis. After a while I sounded like a broken record trying to convince her to write a book about her experiences with Warner Bros.' top woman star and I got nowhere with it. I truly believe that her reluctance stemmed from the fact that the star was still alive and did not take kindly to people writing about her, much in the same way Frank Sinatra was with his friends and co-workers. One had a tendency to try and not ruffle these superstars' considerable feathers or they would know the reason why!

In all phases of a movie production, the people connected with it are certainly a fascinating bunch in their own right.

No Regrets

She had the map of Ireland written all over her face and the dewy freshness of youth that came with the giggle of a teenager and a child-like complexion loaded with freckles that always challenged the make-up department. Yet, in spite of all of this, Jane Bryan's future at Warner Bros. as a young dramatic actress could not have been brighter. To add to the enthusiasm that Jack Warner had for his new contract player, she had the rare, enthusiastic backing and mentoring of no less an icon than Bette Davis. Jane's future was insured.

Jane Bryan was about nineteen years old when she was cast as my older sister in *The Captain's Kid*. She was joining the cast of Guy Kibbee, May Robson, and many fine character actors, and a very handsome young man by the name of Fred Lawrence who was to portray her romantic leading man. I didn't get to meet Jane until we were already a week into shooting the movie.

She had such a warm and genuine personality that all of us just fell in love with her. Unlike most leading ladies, Jane was never concerned with the way she looked. She never fussed with her makeup or wardrobe, but only concentrated on paying attention to our director, Nick Grinde, and her fellow actors.

Jane was not due until later in the day. On this day, I was scheduled for a very dramatic scene with Guy Kibbee. The set was unusually quiet because of the consideration that cast and crew was giving a young child as myself in preparation for this scene. I have done quite a number of crying scenes in my other movies, but I have never been so affected as I was with this one. It lives in my memory to this day because I couldn't quit crying after the director had called CUT. Anita immediately came to my side and close behind her was Jane, who had come in early to witness this scene being shot. When emotionally I had settled down, Jane took me in her arms and said very simply, "You were marvelous!"

Publicity shot from The Captain's Kid, 1936. Jane Bryan, me and Fred Lawrence.

Movie sets differ from production to production and a lot of it has to do with the attitude and persona of the director and the actors. I must say that everything connected with *The Captain's Kid*, from the first day of shooting till the last, was very pleasant and at times a lot of fun. For instance, we were away on location when the scenario called for us to be situated on a deserted island that my Uncle Asa had found on a map and supposedly had some treasure buried on it. I do wish I could remember for sure where we traveled for this location, but if I were to guess I would say Laguna Beach, California. It proved to be a heavenly spot for this young actress because apart from all the exploring that was available between scenes, the site was covered with large and beautiful mother of pearl shells that I carefully gathered and planned to take home with me. To this day, whether it be a lake or ocean, I am at my most peaceful where water is concerned so being on location didn't seem like work at all to me.

Jane was scheduled to be in a later shoot that day so most of the morning she was able to relax, dressed in a polka-dotted sun suit and her hair was left in curlers so that she would look put together later in the scenes she was involved in. Jane was an unusual combination of being a very private person but an extremely social one and that is why no one knew that she was about to celebrate her birthday on that location site. When we broke for lunch, that dear girl had thought ahead of time and brought two immense cakes that were large enough for everyone, crew included, to have a small slice. Because she was very modest, there was not one candle in sight to pronounce that this was a birthday cake. That fact only came out by happenstance when we got back to the studio. The next day it was arranged by a team effort that another cake, this time with candles on it, would be brought out when we broke for lunch and a few gaily wrapped presents accompanied it. It was quite typical of Jane that her freckles were replaced by an embarrassed red flush of shyness when she saw what we had done for her. I never worked with Jane again, but I did visit with her on two of her sets before my contract was up in 1938.

By 1938 Jane Bryan had already earned her stripes in several movies and with each one was gaining a healthy popularity with the movie-going public. She was, for the first time, top billed in a movie called *Girls on Probation*, which cast as her romantic leading man none other than Ronald Reagan. Jane Wyman visited Reagan on the set (just as he did her on the short *Little Pioneer*) and in the interim the situation became the beginning of a close and personal relationship between the two Janes and Ronald Reagan. In that same year all three of them were cast in the very popular movie *Brother Rat* and as a visitor to both sets that Jane Bryan was on, it turned out that that was the very last time that I ever saw her.

On location for *The Captain's Kid* eating Jane's birthday cake.

It is one of the mysteries of life that determines why a friendship can be so very enjoyable but temporary and others that seem to take a firm hold and last a lifetime. The latter would be the case in the friendship between Jane Bryan, Ronald Reagan, and his life partner and second wife, actress Nancy Davis.

You may be wondering what incident occurred in Jane Bryan's life that made her reject a movie career handed to her on a platinum platter without so much as a backward glance or the slightest regrets. His name was Justin Dart and, although he was eleven years older than Jane, as a pair, they fit like a glove. He was not from the world of show business, but was a Walgreen executive and would in subsequent years expand his horizons as a very successful businessman and millionaire. After Jane and Justin married on New Year's Eve in 1939, he eventually took over the Rexall Drug chain in 1945, which was struggling to survive at the time. Jane and Justin then lived in Chicago and Boston, but after a while, because of his various business interests, they found it more convenient to move back to Los Angeles, making their permanent home in Bel Air. They had three children and besides being a devoted mother Jane devoted herself to civic affairs and charities. Being a lover of archeological expeditions, she became so versed in the subject that she was named governor of the Los Angeles History Museum. The Darts became so friendly with "Ronnie and Nancy" that in the very early '60s Justin Dart persuaded Reagan to enter politics. Hard to believe, but at that time Ronald Reagan was registered as a Democrat. Dart further influenced him, much to Nancy's delight, to become a Republican. Dart eventually sold his stake in Rexall and acquired Avon and Duracell and named the conglomerate Dart Industries. When Ronald Reagan became President, the friendship between the two couples never faltered and Justin became an advisor and part of the president's kitchen cabinet. Jane entered Justin's life with ease and satisfaction and when he died in 1984, after many years of married happiness, she lived the next twenty years in the beautiful community of Pebble Beach in northern California.

I cannot explain what prompted me to try and get in touch with Jane after so many years had gone by, but after I obtained her address from a mutual friend I wrote her a short note. Our friend warned me that I just might not hear from Jane because she had been ill for some time and I shouldn't take it personally if I got no reply. She was so right. I had mailed my letter to Jane on March 31, and Jane died on April 8, 2009.

Thank You, Mr. Fonda

In 1938, due to cutbacks Warner Bros made to their contract list of actors, my tenure, along with many others, was brought to an end. That usually spelled disaster for a child star who was beginning to leave the baby stage and starting to enter into a pre-teen phase of life. You know the old expression, "Neither fish nor fowl," and that usually preceded a kid star into the offices of the casting directors and producers and stayed as a blemish until hopefully the ex-moppet started to clean up pretty good and officially entered into an easier casting category of a teenager. For the first month that I was at liberty, so to speak, nothing had changed too much in what I experienced during the summer months at Warners when production had slowed down. That time was usually taken up doing personal appearances, posing for new photographs, doing interviews for magazine articles and for radio. I was still doing much of the same, although not backed or representing Warners.

I was only ten years old at that time and didn't look anywhere like a teenager, but certainly had left the appeal of the baby stage. So it was with a vast sigh of relief that Republic offered me the role as Frieda Inescort's daughter in *Woman Doctor*. I received some very good notices for my work in *Woman Doctor* and even before we had completed it, two offers of work on a steady basis already had come in for me. Both were offers of a contract and they came from MGM and Twentieth Century-Fox studios. For some strange reason, my new agent chose Fox, where America's sweetheart, Shirley Temple, reigned supreme. I have a feeling that his decision was based on what money was offered and Fox delivered the better one of the two so it was a fait d'accompli that after *Woman Doctor* was in the can I started my tenure at Fox.

Of course, I was thrilled when I found out that I was going to work with Shirley and it also appealed to me that I was going to portray a character-type role named Becky in the movie *The Little Princess*. For

Taken at The American Cinema Awards. Edith Fellows, me, Peggy Ann Garner.
Behind us (in the dark), Mrs. Henry Fonda

some strange reason, I always felt more at ease doing dramatic roles rather than cutesy musical ones, even though I had never had an acting lesson in my life, I did have dancing lessons in South Africa starting when I was just a wee one of two years old.

Not being the little princess of the Warners lot anymore, my introduction to Twentieth Century-Fox was as different as night is to day in comparison to when I first arrived at Warners. It felt strange at first being almost a nonentity, but meeting some of the Fox stars was certainly a plus and the "lost" feeling soon dissipated. First of all, Harry Brand was head of Fox publicity at that time and many years after. He saw to it that I had new photos taken, was introduced around the lot and made things generally pleasant for me and Anita. Years later, I became very friendly with Sybil Brand, his wife, and we used to laugh that I would get some of her mail and she would get some of mine just because our first names were not as common as say a Mary or a Betty.

In my book *Five Minutes More* I wrote about meeting Linda Darnell on her very first day on the Fox lot as a brand-new contract player. One of the gentlemen from the press relations department was escorting her around to acquaint her with the physical layout of the studio and along with that process she also got to meet some of her fellow contract players. That became quite a bonanza of opportunity when they entered the commissary at lunchtime. And while we are on the subject of commissaries, every studio had one but I do believe that Fox's Cafe de Paris could lay claim to having been the largest of all of them. Because of its size and just like some restaurants, they were able to install a fan-like but very substantial curtain that could be drawn on a track across the room in order to segregate and insure privacy if so desired for a luncheon-business meeting or a conservative celebration of some kind. This was utilized quite a number of times when Shirley Temple was working at the studio on or around her birthday and in that way she was able to hold one of her parties there. Anyone that ever attended one of her parties knew ahead of time that it was written in stone what the entree would be…her favorite of creamed tuna ensconced in a flaky nest of pastry dough.

In 1938 the lot was busy. I did feel like a real fan when, by chance, I ran across icons like Tyrone Power, Alice Faye, and Henry Fonda and was able to become acquainted with them.

Tyrone Power was breathtakingly handsome and when he smiled at you it didn't matter whether you were ten years old or eighty; your legs would suddenly go very weak at the sight of him. In a different, but very pleasant, way it was a lovely experience meeting Alice Faye. She was one of those actresses that was completely down to earth and actually enjoyed talking to you. You never got the feeling that she had "one foot out the door" or that you were wasting her time. I am not completely sure of this fact but when Shirley Temple and I were shooting *The Little Princess* in 1938, I think that Mr. Fonda was busy working on *Young Mr. Lincoln* or possibly *Jesse James*. In either case, when I asked all three stars if they would autograph a picture of themselves to me they very graciously obliged and those photos were in my possession the very next morning. I have all three of them to this day and they look as fresh as the day they were signed.

Much has been written about Henry Fonda throughout the years. I must say that, personally, in 1938, I found him to be a nice man but a wee bit distant in manner. It was not because he was ignoring you on purpose; you just had the feeling that his mind was busily occupied with something else at the time. Even so, I never felt like I was being slighted and I think the reason for that was that my admiration for him as a fine actor cancelled anything out that approached negativity. That proved so true many, many years later.

When our daughter was about to turn ten years old, my husband Tony and I thought that we would treat her to a different type of experience pre her more conventional birthday party that came a few days later. We saw that Henry Fonda was starring in the play *Our Town* in Hollywood at the Huntington Hartford Theatre on Vine Street (no longer there) and reserved our seats for an evening performance. Before the play started, we gave Toni a very brief rundown of what the play was all about so that when the curtain came up she knew what to expect. We were delighted that she thoroughly enjoyed the play and I thought even though Mr. Fonda certainly would not remember me it would be wonderful if Toni could meet him. I wrote a quick note to him and asked if we could bring her backstage to meet him. Although I honestly had no expectations that that would take place, lo and behold, we were told just to give the star a breather of ten minutes and then Mr. Fonda would see the three of us in his dressing room.

He looked absolutely marvelous and I can't tell you how warm he was to all of us…but especially to Toni. He asked her if *Our Town* was the first play she had seen and if she liked the experience and did she understand it all. He was truly interested in her answers. Then he said that I made him feel quite old when he remembered that I was not much older than my daughter was when we first met at Fox. I could not believe that this man would have remembered that, but he did…so much for the "lack of warmth" in his personality. Just before we left his dressing room, we felt a bit embarrassed asking him rather gingerly if it would be possible if he would sign Toni's program. Before you could blink an eye, this icon of an actor reached over to his table and got a pen and signed the date and a Happy Birthday wish to our daughter, then shook her hand and thanked the three of us for coming to see the play. What a special memory that made.

However, that was not the end of the story. A number of years after that meeting, those of us from The Golden Era of Hollywood were still regularly being feted for the part that we took in the history of Hollywood and we attended the many banquets tossed in our honor. One of the biggest of these was The American Cinema Awards. About the third one that I attended was held on three different levels of a hotel. After the main banquet and the wonderful talent that was brought in to entertain us was over, a lot of us were reluctant to call it a night.

We all went up to the third-floor level and there we were able to sit at the many tables, socialize and order drinks. At my table were two of my closest buddies and fellow kid stars, Peggy Ann Garner and Edith Fellows, and our escorts. We had so much fun discussing the evening's events and the stars that we met that we had never met before. I happened to notice a lovely young woman sitting at the next table and because I didn't recognize her I became curious about who she was. I asked Peg and Edith if they knew her, but they drew a blank as well. She had such delicate features and was quite lovely so we assumed that she was "in the business." Edith then spotted a man who knew just about everyone in Hollywood and as he passed our table we asked him who that lady was. Imagine my surprise when he said that that was Shirley Fonda, Henry's wife. I usually don't barge into people's private conversations, but I just had to tell this young woman how kind her husband had been to my daughter. I walked over to her table and apologized for interrupting her and her friends. She was very gracious when I told her the reason I had come over to her and she said that she would love to hear what I had to say about her Henry. After I finished telling her my experiences that went back to 1938 and progressed to meeting Mr. Fonda again many years later and how he greeted my daughter so warmly, she grabbed my hand, squeezed it and thanked me for telling her such a lovely true story. I am not absolutely certain whether he was still alive at that time (I do think he was) because I have a vague memory of her telling me that she would be sure to remind him of those events and that she had heard it from me that evening.

After my daughter had married and left home (she and her husband lived far away from us…like two blocks away), one day my husband and I were grocery shopping and, lo and behold, who was standing there outside of the checkout stand but Mr. Fonda's son, Peter. I told Tony, my husband, I just couldn't resist going over to him and introducing myself and complimenting him on what a nice man his father had been. Unfortunately, I don't think young Mr. Fonda was "buying it," but one must always remember that family members sometimes remember the worst of times and the "stranger" remembers the best. I am so glad I was the stranger.

I would like to add a passing thought to this chapter because I feel that in its most simplistic form it deals with the loving emotions experienced within a family. When I wrote this poem many years ago, I was inspired by the love and respect that the two loves of my life had for each other…my daughter, Toni Maryanna, and her dad, Anthony Drake. I dedicate this to them.

THE BIRTHDAY PRESENT

A night before my birthday, upon our porch we sat.
My dad and I enjoying a pleasant evening chat.
A neighbor dog was barking, a gentle breeze brushed by.
'Twas then Dad turned and looked at me, a twinkle in his eye.

"My baby, you're sure growing up, tomorrow you'll be ten.
But tonight we'll share a moment that may never come again.
Tomorrow at your party you'll be busy with your friends
And I know you will be tired when the celebration ends.

"So tonight I have a gift for you, it's one that you may choose.
It's very, very precious and it's one you'll never lose."
That was many years ago and now that I'm a wife.
I tell my kids the story of the best gift of my life.

We gather on our front porch, upon a summer's eve.
A neighbor dog is barking and we feel a gentle breeze.
We look up at the evening sky as far as we can see.
And the brightest star that glitters is the gift Dad gave to me.

Lights, Action, Camera

It has been my distinct honor and pleasure to have been directed by the men Hollywood history considered the *crème de la crème*. I have been asked so many times who my favorite director was and why, but the answer to that question has always presented a problem. Their styles and personalities were so diverse that it would be like comparing sardines to ice cream sundaes! Some, unfortunately, never received their well-earned due and now, as I view the Golden Era movies as an adult I often wonder why some of them got the hoopla that they did and still do in the eyes of the new Hollywood historians and the others, for the most part, are rarely mentioned.

Michael Curtiz

If you have read my other two books I am sure that some of you, at times, shook your heads and wondered how the devil a child *dared* to issue an opinion about adults on subjects that youngsters are not supposed to have. In real life adults very rarely asked a child, "What do *you* think?"—but they did with a junior actor. If you reason it this way, the majority of child stars were old souls and did not think in the same or appropriate manner in which the normal child did at that same age, then it might make a bit more sense. To further illustrate this point, let me point out the experience I had while being directed by Michael Curtiz on my very first movie for Warner Bros., *The Little Big Shot*.

I'm not going to deny the well-known fact that Mike had a maniacal temper and when he got angry it was a sight to behold. The veins in his forehead popped out and his eyes bulged as he screamed his displeasure. True enough, that didn't happen often and when it did it was usually for a good reason. His outburst was to generally improve the movie or to help magnify the performance of his actors.

Michael Curtiz directing me in a dramatic scene from my
first WB movie *Little Big Shot*, 1935.

my dog and killed it, as hard as I would try, nothing came from my throat.
Mike called time out and then put me on his lap and gently asked me if I
believed that when we went back to shooting that scene I would accomplish it. I looked him in the eye and softly answered, "I *think* so, Uncle
Mike." He then assured me that he had such confidence that that would
happen he would be right behind me, encouraging me just before I was
to run into the scene screaming. Michael Curtiz was right. I *did* scream
for the first and last time in my life.

So much so did he believe in realism that, earlier, when the assistant
director suggested the scream could always be dubbed in, Mike adamantly
said no. Michael Curtiz got the realism that he wanted because he had
borrowed a long hat pin from wardrobe and used my little buns like a pin
cushion. One might think that very cruel, but I had a rather strange reaction to it. Instead of being hurt, either physically or mentally, I was glow-
ing with pride that I had actually let out a good, loud scream!

Many, many years later, at an autograph session that was held in
North Hollywood, one of the guest stars amongst many was Marc
Lawrence. In my first movie, *The Little Big Shot*, Marc along with Ward

Even as a child I appreciated his direction because he made every-thing so very clear that you knew exactly what he wanted from you and the reason why and in that way you were never left playing any guessing games. He also believed in realism and in my case carried it to extremes.

I had and have a hang-up to this very day that I find it impossible to scream. In 1935, on the set of *The Little Big Shot*, after three takes when I was supposed to run into a scene screaming because a gangster had kicked

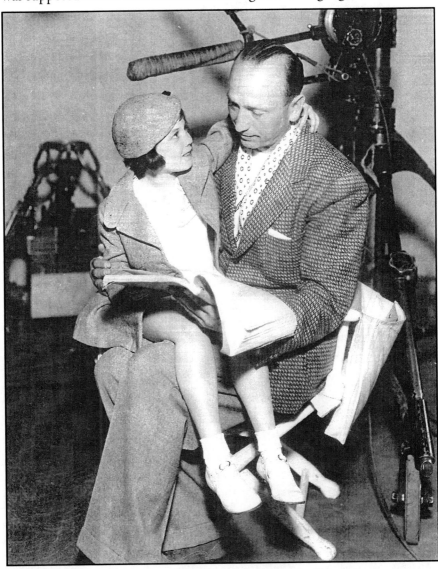

On Michael Curtiz's lap being given assurances that I will be able to scream in next scene in *Little Big Shot*.

Marc Lawrence and Sybil at book signing event.

Bond, J. Carrol Naish and Jack La Rue played the "heavies," as they usually did in most movies. Incongruously, in real life, all four men were very kindhearted gentlemen. Because I hadn't seen Marc in many, many years, we had a wonderful time doing catch up. I learned that he was traveling the country attending these autograph shows and then returning to Palm Springs where he had made his home for years. It's just amazing what people will remember; when we started reminiscing about *The Little Big Shot*, he brought up the subject of Mike using the hat pin to get a scream out of me. I told him that I thought it was mindboggling that he would remember such an incident, but he said it was not *that* mindboggling because he remembered that at the time he wanted to give "Mike Curtiz a knuckle sandwich" for doing that to me. Marc and I kept in contact for a number of years after that.

While I am on the subject of Michael Curtiz, I am going to take the opportunity to discuss something that has been bothering me for years. I am amazed at the many stars that Mike directed who in recent years have been giving interviews on television and mispronouncing his name! I will never forget that Mike, during the shooting of *The Little Big Shot*, told my sister Anita that I was the only person who pronounced his name correctly. I am sure that because I was a child at the time of this incident quite frankly the historians in *this* era are going to take the word of the adult stars, and I really don't blame them. But if one looks at the Hungarian spelling of his name, it is almost phonetically the way I addressed him. It's easy to understand that he changed his first name, which was originally Mano, to Michael, but look at the spelling of his last name, which was Kertesz! Phonetically, I pronounced his last name as "Curr-Tezz."

However, one last thought. That wasn't the only time that Michael Curtiz's name was misspelled and this one was a doozie!! I sang two songs in the movie and they came out in sheet music form after the movie was

Sheet music from *Little Big Shot*. *Note:* Bottom of sheet music
Michael Curtiz's name is misspelled as Mitchell Curtiz.

released. I have included a photo of that sheet music because I'd like you
to take note at the bottom where the credits are listed. You will see that
the movie was directed by…*Mitchell* Curtiz! I feel much better now that
I got all of that off my chest.

I had spent the war years of World War II in the land of my birth, South Africa, through circumstances that I explained in my first book *My Fifteen Minutes*. However, as soon as the war was over, I left Cape Town to return to America in 1947 and within days I was visiting the Warner Bros lot. It was wonderful to get reacquainted with all of the people that I had worked with and permission was given to me to visit Michael Curtiz on the soundstage on which he was directing his newest movie, *The Unsuspected*. Lucky for me they were taking a break and as soon as the message that I was there reached Mike's ears he signaled me to come up on the set.

It was a wonderful reunion and made doubly so because just below the riser of the set sat none other than Claude Rains who dipped his newspaper down that he was reading to witness the reunion. I wonder if he remembered that he and I had been co- guest stars on radio when I was a child. Apparently, he may have because he gave me one of his side-swiped smiles. To this day, I *still* think he is the best scene stealer in Hollywood.

After that, my husband, Tony, and I bumped into Michael Curtiz several times socially at the Brown Derby and other landmarks around town and he looked just like he always did on the set of *Little Big Shot* in 1935…dressed to the nines and right out of *GQ*.

Mervyn LeRoy

Mervyn Leroy earned his formidable stripes as a director-producer in Hollywood in the hardest way imaginable. He experienced the slow climb from near poverty as a child to the dizzying heights of success that he attained because of the decided touch of genius he displayed when first working in the different phases of the motion picture industry.

Going back in time, little Mervyn was only six years old when his hometown of San Francisco suffered the devastating effects of its historic earthquake in 1906. Of the family, only he and his father managed to survive. (His mother apparently had abandoned the family when Mervyn was very little.) They lost everything they had owned and in order just to eke out enough to exist on, little Mervyn sold newspapers and entered talent contests as a singer. Later, he even had an act in vaudeville called Two Kids and a Piano. When that didn't last, he decided to get in touch with his cousin, Jesse Lasky, and move to Los Angeles, although he was barely old enough to face life on his own. He worked many jobs there, from film lab to camera assistant to gag writer and even actor in silent

Sybil and Mervyn Leroy in their directors chairs *I Found Stella Parish*, 1935.

movies. Eventually, he progressed to directing some movies and at last felt that he had found his niche in life. By the time he was twenty years old Mervyn's days of hard luck started to disappear and his earnings started to escalate and so did his reputation at Warner Bros. as a Boy Wonder. He had racked up enough credits so that he could go from directing light-weight comedies to musicals without much effort. Yet, somehow, Mervyn did not feel fulfilled.

At this time there was another young man on the Warner Bros. lot making huge strides in various directions. He had become a successful writer with his first script about a dog called Rin Tin Tin, which became a huge hit as a motion picture, and from then on he advanced consider-ably in various positions until he ultimately headed production. Darryl F. Zanuck soon was fighting the Warner brothers to stop producing all the lightweight musicals they were prone to do and instead make movies that were more of a significant and dramatic nature. When the fights with the front office escalated, Zanuck couldn't stand it any longer and left Warners to ultimately become president of Twentieth Century-Fox.

Shooting a scene from *I Found a Stella Parish* with Jesse Ralph, Sybil, Kay Francis.

Although Mervyn agreed with Zanuck's concept of dealing with realism and social issues that faced the American public every day, he stayed on at Warner Bros. and in his own inimitable and persuasive way directed most of the studio's successful gangster movies and the many scenarios that showed life through the eyes of the underdog.

In 1935 Mervyn was scheduled to direct a movie called *I Found Stella Parish*. It was going to star Warners' top star, Kay Francis, with Ian Hunter as her leading man, and a youngster named Sybil Jason, who had only done one other Warner Bros. movie but was now going to portray Miss Francis's daughter.

As a director Mervyn LeRoy was the dichotomy of Michael Curtiz. He ran a tranquil set, was quiet by nature, and was very sensitive to his actor's emotions. Unlike Curtiz, he did not spend an inordinate amount of time with the placement of props, or slight changes in wardrobe, but concentrated more on the weak or strong characterizations of his actors. I remember asking Anita after I had done a scene if she thought Mr. LeRoy had been pleased with what I had done. She assured me that he had; she then me why I had asked that question. As young as I was and having just had the experience with Michael Curtiz's style of directing, I felt that my new director said very little in the way of directing us. However, it was so subtle in style that as I watch the movie today I am amazed how much he got out of all of us without continually pounding directions our way. This is not to take away from Michael Curtiz. This is just an observation in the different styles that directors had in handling their actors.

Physically, Mervyn was on the shortish and boyish side, but very handsome in face and manner. There are just a handful of directors that I associated with off the set or lot; Mervyn, I'm happy to say, was one of them.

He had the most marvelous beach house in Santa Monica and I would often spend weekends there with him and his wife and a little girl my age. To be honest with you, this is where my memory fails me as I am not quite sure who that little girl was. All I know is she was too old to be Doris and Mervyn's daughter (their own daughter was around one-year-old at this time), but I *do* remember that her name was either Rita or Lita and that I was extremely impressed with a dollhouse that she had. She might possibly have been Harry Warner's adopted daughter, Lita. In any case, I remember Mervyn taking great joy in bundling up us girls on Sunday mornings and taking us for breakfast at his favorite restaurant in Malibu. I believe it is still there; it's right across from the Malibu pier and on the other side of the Pacific Coast Highway. Many years ago, my husband Tony and I stopped there for a sandwich and coffee and they hadn't changed a thing in its western motif and the many autographed pictures of movie stars arranged on the walls. When we didn't go out for breakfast with Mervyn, I remember having my very first taste of French toast at the beach house. When I got back home, I just raved at what a tasty treat that was and Anita made sure that I would have it for breakfast every now and again. My sister was also very happy when Mervyn phoned her and said how impressed he and his family were with my proper upbringing. They noticed that every morning I would place my slippers under their guest bed, fold my pajamas and put them out of sight under my pillow. Anita was always proud of my talents, but I think she was even more so when people commented on what a well-brought-up child I was.

For the movie buff, take a very good look the next time you view *I Found Stella Parish* and the scene where Kay Francis, portraying a stage actress, is on the stage and there are Roman soldiers strategically placed on the set. One of those Roman soldiers who had no lines was Ward Bond. He had just played one of the gangsters who terrorized me in *The Little Big Shot*, but at least he had one line in that movie. Also in a later scene when Kay Francis was supposed to be interviewed by a group of reporters, one of them was a sob sister who didn't even get screen credit: it was the wonderful character actress Mary Treen. One movie later, in *The Captain's Kid,* she portrayed May Robson's maid and my nursemaid. It's fun to keep an eye out for stars who basically earned their stripes the hard way before reaching stardom.

I was in another Kay Francis movie, again portrayed her daughter, *Comet over Broadway*. There is a scene, backstage, where a group of "extra" girls congratulate their leading lady on what a fine job she just did. One even had a short line and that girl was...Susan Hayward!

The last time that I saw Mervyn was at a historic event, one that I feel deserves a long explanation for you movie history buffs.

At 10:30 a.m., on October 6, 1977, a very special event was held to honor fifty years of talking pictures. A carefully selected group of Warner Bros. stars were gathered on Stage 6 at KTLA, which was the original site of where they shot *The Jazz Singer*. After thanking everyone for coming and reminding them of the historical facts of what took place on that site where the very first talking movie, starring Al Jolson, was made, we were then informed what the rest of the celebration would be like. Several busses drew up to the building on Sunset Boulevard and several groups of us boarded our transportation that was going to take us to the famous nightclub and dance hall The Hollywood Palladium. Tony and I were sitting next to William Demarest and he kept us hysterical with his remarks about the Warner brothers and some of the stars that he personally had worked with. As some of you who are familiar with the famous site, The Palladium, you must know how very large it was and is. On this day there were multiple tables draped with white linen tablecloths. Centered in the middle

Sybil and Leroy with cub sent by a fan and named Sybil.

of the "dance floor" was a riser that contained the gentlemen that were going to make the important remarks of the day and also the introductions of the special guest stars. No less than Jack Valenti, Ted Ashley (who at that time was Chairman of the Board at Warner Bros.) reminded everyone why they were there and how, through their careers, they played a significant part in the celebration of this day. At each table we were given a commemorative first-day issue stamp proclaiming the fifty years of sound. The festivities started with Hal Kanter and Jack Valenti introducing each and every one of us with a little mini-background of who we were. This took the majority of the day and just to give you an idea of the list of the people that they introduced, it was a bonanza of silent stars, stars of the '30s, and many directors and producers.

Sitting at our table was my dear friend Pat O'Brien, my fellow co-star Jane Wyman, and Bobby Gordon, who played Jolson as a youngster in *The Jazz Singer* and who just happened to be Tony's and my beach buddy almost every weekend in Santa Monica. Bobby was now the spitting image of the mature Al Jolson even to the deep, deep tan he kept all round the year.

Amazingly, there were several stars of the silent era, like Doris Kenyon, Carmel Myers and Jetta Goudal, nodding their heads as Misters Kanter or Valenti spoke of some incidents that happened in the silent days. Seated amongst some of the stars were also well-known producers like Sol Lesser and Howard Koch and on the other side of the Palladium famous directors of the thirties sat reminiscing with each other. Amongst them were giants like George Seaton, George Cukor, Mervyn LeRoy, Alan Crosland and Nick Grinde (whom I hadn't seen in years). We even had some "new faces" that attended this event.

A very funny thing happened when I was introduced by Hal Kanter, something that got a huge laugh from the audience. After he announced my name, he issued my background as "Sybil Jason...Warners' first child." There was a long pause and he put up his hand and apologized if he gave the impression that I was Jack Warners' daughter. He then mentioned my name again and repeated that I was Warner Bros.' first child star and he said, looking at me, "She doesn't seem to have changed a bit since then." That brought the "new face" of Natalie Wood to her feet to get a good look at me. A number of years later her husband Bob Wagner would introduce 300 of us individually at the American Cinema Awards.

After the event broke up, a lot of us adjourned to the lobby of the Palladium to await the arrival of our private cars that had been parked near KTLA. There were some rounded cement castings on the floor of the lobby that held plants and I saw Mervyn had sat down on one of them. He looked quite tired, but his face broke out into a grin when Tony and I approached him. We did manage to spend a little time together before it was announced that his transportation had arrived. After a hug or two and a handshake to Tony, he got up to go to his car. After he was gone, I mentioned to my husband how amazed I was what a great memory Mervyn had of our days on *Stella Parish*.

This event took place on October 6, 1977, and, sadly and incongruously, almost exactly ten years later, Mr. Mervyn LeRoy died on September 13, 1987, of...Alzheimer's disease.

Busby Berkeley

There were two outstanding dance director-choreographers at Warner Bros. in the 1930s and those two talented gentlemen were Busby Berkeley and Bobby Connelly. One would think that there would be much jockeying around for position to be top dog, but they had a most compatible collaboration on several movie projects due to a dramatic real-life experience one of them was going through at the time. Of the two, Busby

Berkeley, historically, has become uppermost in Hollywood history.

I have heard it said by my friends Judy Garland and Ann Miller that Buzz was an out-and-out terror to work for. I don't doubt that to be true because I have heard it from other people as well, but as far as I was concerned he was precise in his wants, but quite easy on me. I assume that's because I was a child at the time.

I starred in four Warner Bros. Technicolor shorts from 1936 through late 1937. Of the four, my favorite was *Changing of the Guard*. The color was and is absolutely magnificent and was at its peak during a dream sequence that featured the Kings Grenadier Guards dressed in their red and plaid uniforms. Actually, those grenadiers

Busby Berkeley directing Al Jolson and Sybil in their musical duet from *The Singing Kid*, 1936.

eventually turned into the Buzz Berkeley dance girls who backed me up in a precision military tap dance. It's an amazing fact that the girls and I never got together until the very day of shooting that sequence, but when we did, it went off like clockwork. For a few days preceding the shoot, Bobby Connelly worked with the girls and Buzz worked with me separately. Only Bobby got credit for directing that sequence (which he did once the girls and I got together) because in 1935 Mr. Berkeley was involved in a DUI in Santa Monica in which three people were killed and he was up for manslaughter. Warner Bros. wanted to keep him busy in between trials, but gave him no credit on several projects. The one was the Technicolor short *Changing of the Guard* and the next one was the 1936 Al Jolson-starrer *The Singing Kid*.

Before I get into that story, I'd like to tell you an interesting fact that ties Bobby Connelly to *Changing of the Guard* years before doing the Warner Bros. short subject. The very last show that Florenz Ziegfeld produced on Broadway starred Mitzi Mayfair doing a precision military tap dance in *Ziegfeld Follies of 1931* to the song "Changing of the Guards," and it was directed by Bobby Connelly!

Buzz never got tired of saying that I was the only one who had proof that he directed and choreographed some musical sequences of *The Sing-*

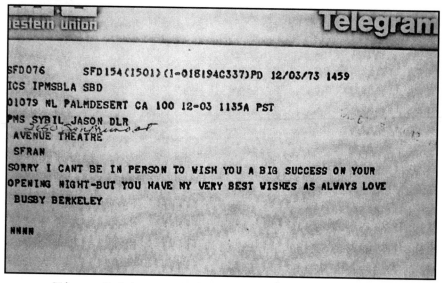

SFD076   SFD154(1501)(1-018194C337)PD 12/03/73 1459
ICS IPMSBLA SBD
01079 NL PALMDESERT CA 100 12-03 1135A PST
MS SYBIL JASON DLR
AVENUE THEATRE
SFRAN
SORRY I CANT BE IN PERSON TO WISH YOU A BIG SUCCESS ON YOUR
OPENING NIGHT-BUT YOU HAVE MY VERY BEST WISHES AS ALWAYS LOVE
BUSBY BERKELEY

NNNN

Telegram Berkeley sent to Sybil on her lecture tour opening night
in 1973 San Francisco.

ing Kid. You see, he had several trials going on due to the car accident that
had not been legally resolved yet so although he was still working for
Warner Brothers he did some projects without credit. The proof that Buzz
was talking about was several stills that I had showing him directing Al
Jolson and myself in our duet in the wharf scene. By the way, the location
of that scene was the same one as the opening shot of Ron Howard, as
Opie, and Andy Griffith walking along with fishing poles on *The Andy
Griffith Show.* As even further proof of Buzz's directorial work, I had home
movies that my guardians took showing him directing Jolie and me in our
song, "You're The Cure For What Ails Me," first in rehearsals in our street
clothes and then in make-up and wardrobe. Now, years later, some more
home movies have been discovered that Harold Arlen took as well while
we were on that location and I'm hoping that Buzz got to see them before
he left this world of ours.

As I have explained previously, by 1938 the roster of Warner Bros.
contract stars were dwindling fast and if they weren't given their pink slips
outright they were given below standard movies they would never have
previously accepted to star in. Cruelly, this happened to Kay Francis, who
for a long time was Warner Bros.' *numero uno* leading star and most popular
leading lady with the movie-going public. As I understand it, Miss Francis
would not take a drop in salary, but instead decided to take any produc-

tion that they handed her on a very tarnished platter. Enter a movie called *Comet over Broadway*. Bette Davis and Miriam Hopkins both turned the movie down and, as director of the movie, so did Michael Curtiz, William Keighley and Edmund Goulding. As for me, my days at Warners were numbered because I was no longer Warner Bros.' baby star. Janet Chapman was originally cast as Kay Francis's daughter, but my beloved Kay, who was in a precarious position herself at Warners, came to bat for me and asked if she could have Sybil Jason in the part of Jackie, her daughter. This was so like this lady. Anyone who knew her well knew she was on hand at all times for the underdog! This was *not* a good movie. It had a wonderful cast, with Ian Hunter, Donald Crisp and Minna Gombell, but it was not enough to override a weepy soap opera. Surprisingly enough, the screenplay was by Mark Hellinger. It was finally decided that the directorial job would go to choreographer and dance director Busby Berkeley and by this time he was in no position to turn down any movies after having just gone through his trial for manslaughter. In later years, Buzz handled the direction of drama beautifully, but in 1938, for *Comet Over Broadway*, nothing really jelled. Buzz was in a depressed mood and I guess everyone else was as well considering the plight of their careers.

Although Busby Berkeley had been married seven times, we talked very often over the phone. Sometimes his wife (his last one) would answer

Busby Berkely directing Al Jolson and Sybil in musical sequence
from *The Singing Kid*, 1936

the phone and we had some very nice conversations; mostly about how happy they both were by making their home in Palm Springs and that at last he seemed to be living the peaceful life of a retired gentleman. She always made me feel welcome to call at any time because his spirits would lift each time I called. He may have been content to be a retired gentleman, but he still enjoyed talking about "the old days" so we did spend some time phoning back and forth. Like all of us who had careers in the movies, one room in our homes was usually devoted to memorabilia and autographed and framed pictures of the stars we knew and worked with. During our conversations, he would say, "It seems like yesterday we were rehearsing the song from *The Singing Kid*. Now I stare at a picture right in front of me on my wall of us taken at that time that you were kind enough to send to me," then he added, rather sadly, "Now so much time has passed."

Years ago, when I was doing a lecture on my career at a theatre in San Francisco, I invited Buzz to be my special guest on opening night. He sent me a lovely telegram regretting that he wasn't able to come. Later on I found out that at that particular time he was not a well man. Although the movie *Comet Over Broadway* will never go down in history as a movie one must not miss, it was an honor to have worked with the genius of choreography and dance, director Busby Berkeley, in various movies, whether he was credited for them or not. I am especially happy to see that the movie historians of late are giving Buzz the due he dearly deserves. It may have been long overdue, but as the saying goes…better late than never.

I have been known, from time to time, to have a stubborn streak in me, but, in my defense, may I say that it has almost always been for a specific reason. This is one of those times. As you will soon see, this section of *Lights, Camera, Action* will be doing double-duty in that I am combining two directors into one chapter. I spent a lot of time mulling this decision over because it had been suggested to me more than once that instead of brooding over what to write about these two gentleman I should just delete them and get on with the rest of it. Hollywood had already done that to them and I refuse to be a partner in the crime of deletion. True enough, this will be a very short section, but I'm sure that my readers will forgive me and perhaps even enjoy what little information that will come forth about these two talented gentlemen.

Sidney Salkow

After my tenure was over at Warner Bros., I was lucky enough to have been almost immediately offered a part in a movie at Republic. True enough, Republic was not near the caliber of Warner Bros., MGM or Twentieth Century-Fox studios, but there were other compensations. Republic was essentially known as the home of the Western and, of course, their biggest stars were John Wayne, Roy Rogers and Gene Autry. However, in 1939, one of their first non-Western movies starred actors who were known for their dramatic portrayals at other major studios in a movie called *Woman Doctor*. When Anita and I saw the cast list, we were delighted because it was going to be almost like home week for me. For the second time in my career I was going to portray the daughter of Frieda Inescort. However, both of our roles in this movie were going to be decidedly different than the ones we had in Warner Bros.' *The Great O'Malley*. In that movie our family was very poor and I was the crippled daughter of Frieda and Humphrey Bogart. In *Woman Doctor*, Ms. Inescort was a dedicated but high-society doctor and I was a pretty spoiled brat due to not having too much quality time with my mother because of her dedication to her job. The second cast member who was also an alumnus of Warner Bros. was Claire Dodd, who portrayed the *femme fatale* in *The Singing Kid*. Claire, who was the nicest woman you could imagine, was going to repeat her role as a *femme fatale* in *Woman Doctor*.

The producer of *Woman Doctor* was a top-flight executive, Sol Siegel, who went onto a brilliant career at Twentieth Century-Fox. He was the producer of *A Letter To Three Wives* and *Three Coins in the Fountain*, both of which were nominated for Oscars for Best Picture of the Year, *Gentlemen Prefer Blondes* with Marilyn Monroe and Jane Russell and *High Society* with Bing Crosby, Frank Sinatra and Grace Kelly.

The director of *Woman Doctor* was Mr. Sidney Salkow. Most of you won't be familiar with his name, even though he did direct over fifty movies, an interesting potpourri of genres ranging from swashbucklers to musicals. A lot of the very talented and A1 directors did not have the talent or facility to switch from one genre to another and much preferred to specialize in the ones that they felt most comfortable with, but Sidney tried them all. Some of you TV buffs may recognize his name if you are devotees of *The Addams Family* because he directed quite a few of their segments.

Making *Woman Doctor* was a very nice experience for me. This was not only because I knew and had worked with some of the cast members, but because Sidney seemed to pay me extra attention. I am sure the reason was because he himself had been a child actor in the theatre in New York and could relate to my being a child actress.

When we had some break time in between setups, somehow the subject of Michael Curtiz came up. I told Sidney about my experiences with him. At that time I had no idea that Sidney's parents were Hungarians like Curtiz. He told me that after they had come to this country most of his family, in one way or the other, eventually landed up in show business. Once I learned that Sidney had two brothers, I wrongly assumed that they had become actors, but this gave my director a good laugh. He stated that neither one of them would have been capable of uttering a single line, but he proudly informed me that they were super talent agents. As for their father, he earned his living as a tailor for the very famous Western Costume Company. As a matter of fact, you can see the exterior of that building in the movie *What Ever Happened to Baby Jane?* when Bette Davis in a scene goes to pick up a costume for herself.

Sidney was a "gentle" director and was the dichotomy of his volatile fellow Hungarian director, Michael Curtiz. He was always well-prepared in the mornings as to what he wanted accomplished for that day's shoot and guided his actors gently in that direction. As happens on most movie sets, if something went wrong Sidney was the calming influence on everyone, whether they be the actors or the crew members.

There was a scene in the movie where, in anger, I take off on my horse and the speed we take gets out of hand. Naturally, a double did the riding part of it for me, but in the script I am supposed to fall off the horse and hit my head on a rock. This is where the magic of editing comes in. You see my double falling off the horse, but what you *don't* see in a separate scene is off camera someone pushing me into the scene where my head lands on a pretty good-sized rock. Unfortunately, I landed so hard that I eventually got a big lump on my temple. Sidney was the first person to run over to see if I was all right and quickly ordered that a doctor see me immediately. Of course, I was just fine with just a bruise on my temple, which was covered up by make-up for the later scenes.

One never knows what the future will hold. When we all said goodbye after the movie was finished, I never realized that I would not see Sidney ever again except for a few phone calls in the 1950s. By this time I was a married lady and my husband Tony and I had just taken over an apartment that Rock Hudson had. As a matter of fact, when we first looked at the apartment and the manager-owner took us in to see it, Rock was still in bed sleeping.

We saw Rock quite a number of times after we had moved in. When he came to check to see if we received any of his mail, we got to talking and Rock mentioned that one of his first directors was Sidney Salkow. When he heard that Sidney had been my director at one time as well, but that I hadn't seen him in years, he gave me Sidney's phone number. It was lovely talking to him and because he was such a warm person it didn't seem like any time had passed since making our movie. As it is in this business, for some reason or the other we never got together and the very next time I made any contact with he or his family he had passed away. The incongruity of the whole thing was he lived within walking distance of our home in Studio City. One day I had been looking through our local newspaper and came across, in the Obituaries, the name Sidney Salkow. The funeral parlor was named where Sidney was taken and I left a message for his wife with my condolences and my phone number. It was but a few hours later when I received a phone call from his dear wife Patricia and she was kind enough to tell me that her husband spoke fondly of me many times. How very strange life is; not only did the Salkows live within walking distance of my home, but Sidney headed the film program at Cal State Northridge where my daughter Toni was attending college. She was the very first female sports editor in the history of the junior college at the same time that Sidney lectured there. It was a privilege to have known and worked with such a lovely gentleman and a fine and sensitive director as Mr. Sidney Salkow.

Nick Grinde

For the readers of both of my previous books, by now you are all familiar with the main purpose of my writings, which is and has been my "personal behind-the-scenes" stories of the Hollywood icons I was fortunate enough to work with or just knew very well. Because of this theme, I rarely had to do much research on them except to be accurate in regards to their birth, wedding and death dates because the stories essentially came from my experiences with them. However, if my personal experiences were limited to just the length of time it took to make a movie, my information would also be quite limited…but hopefully not dismissive.

I was completely stunned and saddened by the lack of information that is now available through the Internet for Nick Grinde. In fact, I was so intrigued by this lack of information available on a gentleman that was part of the motion picture industry from 1928-1945 that I explored everything that the computer had on Nick Grinde. One after the other his

Nick Grande helming scene from *The Captain's Kid* in directors chair.
Man above in white shirt Oscar winner cinemaphotograpger Ernie Haller

life and career only amounted to the same few sentences that summed up his whole career and life. There was no inkling into this gentleman who had directed over 57 movies and tutored Broadway stage directors in the techniques of moviemaking. On the other hand, to be very realistic, Nick Grinde was not in the same category of a Michael Curtiz, a Sydney Pollack or a John Huston. However, besides his directorial credits, his talents were widespread. He was one of the writers for Laurel and Hardy's *Babes in Toyland* and wrote many short stories that were published on a fairly regular basis by such pictorials as *The Saturday Evening Post*.

In 1936 I really enjoyed being directed by Mr. Grinde in *The Captain's Kid*. What struck me the most about him was his heavy concentration on our every move while shooting a scene. One would think that this heavy concentration would be quite intimidating, but it wasn't because as actors we just *knew* that he cared very deeply how you were coming across. If it was a scene that involved two or three actors, one never really knew if it was you or someone else who could have done better in the scene because he always used the phrase "I think we can do better. Let's try it again," but giving no clue as to who had "goofed."

As a child star it was almost written in stone that you would have a crying scene in every movie that you did and *The Captain's Kid* was no exception. As a matter of fact, I am probably more proud of the crying scene that I did in the jail cell with Guy Kibbee than in any other movie that I ever did. The reviewers always pointed out this scene after seeing the movie and when it was shown just recently it was commented that it had to go down in Hollywood history as the most emotional sequence of any child star up to that date. I don't know whether it was because of the "comfortable feeling" that I had with Nick Grinde as a director or a combination of things that made that crying sequence so very realistic to do, but for the very first time in my career I was unable to stop crying after the cameras quit rolling. It was unbelievably quiet after the director called CUT and then what was completely unusual is Nick Grinde left the set and no one knew where he went or why.

After about ten minutes, the assistant director went to look for him and found him seated in a dark corner with his head in his hands. Apparently, the a.d. asked him if he was all right and Nick Grinde just waved him off and said he would soon come back to the set and for him to just call a break for the time being. When he returned to the set for the next scene and saw that I was all calmed down and ready for the next scene, he put his arms around me but didn't say a word. Ernie Haller (Oscar-winning cinematographer) asked our director if that last scene had been "a take" and all that Nick Grinde would say was, "What do *you* think!"

In some of the sparse data that the computer gave on my director, it was written that he was married to actress Marie Wilson. True enough, she often came down to the set or joined Nick for lunch in the Green Room and what a lovely and warm lady she was. But it was understood

On location with May Robson, Sybil and Nick Grinde. *The Captain's Kid*, 1936.

that although they lived together, they never took that trip down the aisle. Perhaps the computer data has much more information than I do, but all I do remember is that Mr. Grinde always introduced her to me or anyone else as "Miss Wilson," but never as "my wife" or "my girlfriend."

The very last day of *The Captain's Kid* was also the very last day that I saw Nick Grinde until 1977 (exactly forty years later!). It was at the history-making event of the 50th anniversary of talking pictures. As I have explained earlier, it was an opportunity for reunions with people that one had not seen in years. When all the introductions had been made and the accolades were presented about us individually, I made my way over to the other side of the ballroom of The Palladium where most of the directors had been seated. I wanted to see Nick Grinde so much. Naturally, like all of us, he had aged considerably and was in a wheelchair, but there was nothing wrong with his memory. We reminisced about the making of *The Captains Kid* and when I told him that he was one of my favorite directors, he got tears in his eyes. He turned around to say something to the lady who was in charge of his wheelchair and said, "As far as I am concerned, she was the very best of the child stars." That lady was a lovely Korean-American actress and *this* time he introduced me to his wife, Hazel Shon Grinde, who obviously had made him a very happy man. That made me happy for them both and in turn made it easier to take when not two years later I heard that Mr. Nick Grinde had passed away. I will always remember him as a lovely gentleman, a sensitive director and, in his last years, a contented human being.

To this day I find it fascinating how diversified the personalities of my directors were both in manner and in dress. Of course, it is not because any of them ever came into work looking like the absentminded professor or even the fictional television detective named Columbo. To the contrary. But, in everyday life, some of these gentlemen took more pride in their appearance than the others did, yet *never* in an obviously narcissistic way.

There were three of them that came to work every morning looking like they just came out of the pages of *GQ* and with the demeanor to match...yet there was one exception to the rule. Although Michael Curtiz had the impeccable appearance of the others, the whole picture was a bit lopsided because he always retained his volatile personality and that certainly made him unique but no lesser a talent. The three gentlemen out of the pages of *GQ* were Curtiz, Walter Lang, and William Keighley.

William Keighley

If I were a casting director I would have given William Keighley the roles of a Harvard-educated lawyer or a judge because he had such a distinguished look about him. He had a beautiful speaking voice, which stemmed from his experience as a stage actor in his earlier years spent in New York. I think his voice had a lot to do with him relocating to Hollywood when sound came to the movies and he was hired by Warner Bros. as a dialogue and assistant director in 1932. In later years, in part because his voice was so mellifluous, he took over the job of host and commentator on the very popular radio drama show The *Lux Radio Theatre* from no less than Cecil B. DeMille.

The semi-documentary short *A Dream Comes True* shows all of the guest arrivals at the preview of *A Midsummer's Night Dream* in 1935. According to the commentator, it was the biggest gathering of stars ever to attend a movie opening in motion picture history. It certainly was exciting for me as it was my very first time at a movie premiere, which, for the most part, was attended by every Warner Bros. star, producer, and director, and it was the very first time that I saw William Keighley, who directed *A Midsummer's Night Dream*. It was a brief meeting.

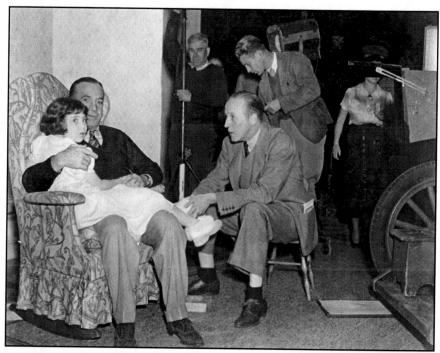

William Keighley directing Sybil and Al Jolson in *The Singing Kid*, 1936.

Less than a year later, he was named director of the movie in which I was to co-star with the iconic talent of Al Jolson, *The Singing Kid*. As young as I was, I always had the feeling that Jolie, who I adored, felt uncomfortable in the medium of motion pictures. First of all, he had to learn to limit his physical actions for the camera whereas on stage he was free to give full vent into his songs to both his and his audience's pleasure. Perhaps some other directors would have had the sensitivities to know how to make things as easy as possible for Al Jolson, but for sure William Keighley certainly did. Without argument, Jolie took Keighley's direction seriously and even asked questions of him, which up until then was unheard of from Al Jolson. I personally felt him relax when he and I did our song on the wharf, "You're the Cure for What Ails Me," written by those two giants of music Harburg and Arlen, who, not three years later, went on to compose the songs for my friend Judy Garland in *The Wizard of Oz*. As I have written in my Buzz Berkeley chapter, William Keighley actually stepped aside to allow Buzz to direct that wharf scene, but in all the dramatic scenes Mr. Keighley was our guiding light. As a director he had a very light and unobtrusive touch which suited Mr. Jolson just right and allowed Beverly Roberts to feel just a little more confident on her debut appearance on screen. Having had only experience as a stage actress, she was now leading lady to the iconic Jolson. Beverly always felt a bit lopsided trying to learn to calm down her movements for the camera as did her leading man. When I was an adult, Beverly confided in me that she never was able to "take" to Mr. Jolson. So many people were intimidated with Jolie; he exuded so much confidence that it took away any identity that others around may have had of themselves. William Keighley realized this and tried to cater to people who were not quite sure of themselves. Our director, I am sure, would have made a wonderful psychologist had he chosen to be one.

The making of the movie went very smoothly with no problems that I could see. Mr. Keighley was not fond of having many visitors to the set as he felt it was a disruption in our schedule and sometimes they overstayed their welcome. However, there was definitely an exception to that rule: Mr. Jack Warner often visited the set when Mr. Jolson had scenes because he was such a devotee of his singing star. One day, in between scenes, Jolie was explaining about what happened on stage when he was singing a particular song and as if to illustrate it better, he started to sing it. Jack Warner was in his glory and joined in singing the song with Mr. Jolson. All of a sudden, Jolie stopped singing and held up his hand. He looked at his boss, Mr. Warner, and said, "Jack, I promise never to tell you how to produce a movie if you promise *never* to try and sing a song!" All I can say is it's a good thing that remark was made by Al Jolson; otherwise, it could have led to a donnybrook or at least a pink slip!

The last time I saw William Keighley was at the preview of *The Singing Kid*, but I did have many glimpses of him walking the lot or having lunch in the Green Room.

After I had returned to America in 1947, having spent the war years in South Africa, I made an extra special effort to try and get in touch with as many people as I could that I had worked with or had been very friendly with. William Keighley and his lovely actress wife, Genevieve Tobin, were two. I managed to get their home phone numbers from columnist Louella Parsons. They graciously gave me their address and invited me to their home for lunch the next day. I must explain to you how unusual this is. Hollywood has a very short memory and usually if one has not been in the limelight for three to six months maximum one is faced with the feeling of being a leper. I had not worked in Hollywood from 1941 to

1947, but I have been a very lucky woman in that I have never felt put upon or belittled. This was very much the case that day at the Keighley-Tobin household. They had a beautiful home right in back of the Beverly Hills Hotel on Tower Drive and their furnishings were right out of England; beautiful antiques and comfy upholstered furniture. There was not a maid in sight, but when it was time for lunch (which turned out to be an exquisite high tea), Mrs. Keighley rolled out a tea tray groaning with many goodies like finger sandwiches, scones, pastries, and the ever-present and nonstop flowing tea while we continued on with our catch-up conversation. From what I could gather, he was still directing movies, but was very disillusioned with the medium. (He quit after his last assignment, The Master of Ballantrae, which starred a very tired Errol Flynn in 1953.)

I *do* remember both Mr. and Mrs. Keighley commenting how much they liked the French people and France, but on that day in their home they never hinted that that's where they would have liked to live when he retired from the business. He had been with CBS radio for quite a while, but in 1965, when he retired, that's exactly what they did. They moved to Paris. They must have relocated back to America one time or another because, according to his public statistics, William Keighley died in New York City of a pulmonary embolism on the June 24, 1984. I am so glad and grateful that we spent that lovely day on Tower Drive speaking of pleasant things past which makes my memory of *that* day to *this* day really quite wonderful.

Walter Lang

I met Walter Lang in the most roundabout way possible, yet it was certainly a very glamorous and fun journey. The whole story is in my book, *Five Minutes More*. There is a chapter called A Potpourri Of Talent and within that chapter there is a subtitle called "There Is Nothing Like A Dame," which featured four wonderful ladies named Joan Blondell, Glenda Farrell, Marion Davies and Carole Lombard. What has this to do with a gentleman by the name of Walter Lang? In a brief way I will give you a rundown.

It was at a lawn party given at the home of Claudette Colbert that my sister and I met the Carole Lombard's best friend. We were talking to Miss Colbert when a very nice-looking woman joined us. Our hostess introduced us to this lady, named Fieldsie (obviously a nickname), and when she heard my name she became extremely complimentary about my work at Warner Bros. and wanted to know what I was working on now. At the time I had just started on the movie *The Great O'Malley*, where, unbelievably, I was billed over Humphrey Bogart. She said she and her husband would be sure to see it when it came out because they had seen most of my films. Anita and I noticed that this lady seemed to be very popular with everyone because many people stopped by to say hello to her and she very graciously introduced me and my sister to them if we didn't happen to know them.

A few months had gone by since that garden party and I was one of many celebrities that taking part in a benefit appearance at the famous Shrine Auditorium in Los Angeles. As was the usual routine, all the guest stars were gathered backstage waiting for their name to be called to make their appearance on stage. While we waited, who should approach us with a huge smile and a warm greeting but Fieldsie. She said it was quite a coincidence because only the night before, at home, she and her husband were talking about what a fine little actress I was, especially in my dramatic scenes. She couldn't stay too long with us because she had to get back to her friend, Carole Lombard, who was also waiting to be called on the stage, but she would soon get in touch with us and make arrangements for all of us to get together.

Besides being best friends with Lombard, Fieldsie was the wife of none other than director Walter Lang! We associated with many people on the Warner Bros lot, but it was unusual that we became so close to the Langs, who seemed to like my guardians and me so much we spent some lovely times at their charming home in Beverly Hills and some fun weekends at their mountain retreat in Lake Arrowhead.

I must remind you that Hollywood is a small but whirlwind community and most of the inhabitants are busy continuously going from job to job, studio to studio, so it is quite difficult to keep up regular social activities like one does in "civilian life." Sadly, so it went with the Langs.

By 1939, I had already left Warner Bros. and was now in the middle of finishing a movie at Republic. Two offers for a contract for me came in from MGM and Fox. My agent chose Fox and you can just imagine my excitement to learn that my first picture there would be in a movie starring Shirley Temple called *The Little Princess*. More surprises were in store there for me. The director of that movie was going to be none other than Walter Lang!

It was a joy being directed by Walter. I must say that even though we had been friends before I ever came to Fox and Shirley was the star of the movie, Walt never played favorites. It was obvious that he liked his whole cast, which also included Anita Louise, Richard Greene, Ian Hunter, Arthur Treacher and Mary Nash. Although he was precise in his direction, at the same time, he was also a most laidback gentleman. However, one giveaway when Walter was especially pleased with how a scene went and after he had said "Cut.....Print it" was the biggest Cheshire cat grin that would come on his face. That always gave me such a warm feeling knowing that we all did good!

Our second movie together was *The Blue Bird*, also starring Shirley Temple. I do not want to repeat what I have already written in my first book, but because this following story involves Walter Lang, I will briefly repeat an edited version of what happened after *The Blue Bird* was finished and scheduled for its premiere showing.

Prior to being cast in the Maeterlink story, I must tell you that due to the excellent reviews that I got for my portrayal of Becky in *The Little Princess*, a rumor circulated that Mrs. Temple would never allow me to do another movie with Shirley. Whether this was true or not, it wasn't long before the publicity department of Fox issued out many bulletins that read that I would be cast as the little crippled girl, Angela Berlingot, in *The Blue Bird*.

My sister and I were very relieved at the news but, unfortunately, it was soon watered down when we first saw the script. My part was little more than a bit part. I had a scene in the beginning of the movie and a short scene at the end, but we did take great hope that the scene where Angela discovers she can walk would make up for the brevity of the role. I want to make it clear that neither Anita nor I had ever thought that I would get the same treatment that I got at Warner Bros. at Fox, but it was still a shock that I was ordered to play Shirley's part and read her lines with my back to the camera when the studio was testing various actors and actresses for parts in the movie. As bad as this was, we realized that we were in no position to complain about it so I did as I was told.

However, the straw that broke the camel's back came when instead of the studio phoning us with the details of the preview of *The Blue Bird* and what time we should be ready to attend, one week before the preview was slated we got a phone call from Walter asking us to come to his office at our convenience. Walter was our friend and although we didn't have any real misgivings about this meeting, Anita still felt a bit skittish about it considering that even before the shooting of the movie began I had less than encouragement from anyone on that lot.

Walter's greeting to us was, as usual, very warm and gracious, but it was obvious he was visibly uncomfortable. He hem and hawed for the longest time, but then reluctantly got to the point of the meeting. But before he did, he prefaced his remarks with a personal statement. In his opinion, he felt that the scene where Angela Berlingot discovers she can walk was the finest one in the movie. Walter then dropped the bombshell. He said that his hands were tied but he had to edit out my "big scene" because Mrs. Temple had told Mr. Zanuck that if that scene was left in she and Shirley would walk out of the studio. Anita and I had decided that we didn't need any further humiliations and we did not attend the preview. The very next day after the preview three-dozen beautiful roses were delivered to my home with a card that read: "Sent with our deepest love and respect. Walter and Fieldsie Lang."

Walter went on to direct some of best musicals to come out of Fox and many of the most popular ones still being shown on television: *Tin Pan Alley, Moon Over Miami, Coney Island, There's No Business like Show Business* and, one of my personal favorites, *The King and I.* When Walter Lang passed away in 1972, he and his beloved Fieldsie had been ecstatically happily married for thirty-five years with nary a blot on either one of their characters. They were such a class act.

Note:

Please note that I have not forgotten one of my directors who guided Pat O'Brien, myself, Humphrey Bogart, Ann Sheridan, Frieda Inescort and Donald Crisp in the Warner Bros 1937 movie *The Great O'Malley.* I have not included William Dieterle in this particular book or chapter on my directors only because I wrote about him quite extensively in *My Fifteen Minutes* in the chapter entitled "Oh Daddy," which highlighted Humphrey Bogart and the behind-the-scenes making of *The Great O'Malley.* Granted, Mr. Dieterle was one of the finest directors in the Golden Era and beyond, and if one looks up his motion picture credits you will find that they are first class, but I do admit that he did have many personal issues that made working for him quite difficult.

I also have not mentioned two other directors that I had because my experiences with them were either way too short to write about or in one case the only really painful experience that I ever had in my motion picture career. If every actor or actress could make that last statement of experiencing just *one* painful experience, I think we should deem ourselves very lucky...I certainly do!

I almost didn't write about this next gentleman because, technically, I could not claim him as one of my directors. However, he did decidedly play a big part in making a rather tense movie set livable with his voice of reason.

Irving Rapper

In Hollywood history you will not see Mr. Rapper being mentioned as walking shoulder to shoulder with all of the iconic directors from the Golden Age of Hollywood, but he definitely belongs there. I feel that all that is necessary to perk up your interest in him is to mention a few of the movies that he directed and you'll see he guided some masterpieces and gently but persuasively mentored the actors that starred in them. Who has not seen *Now, Voyager, The Corn is Green,* and *The Glass Menagerie,* to name a few? Irving Rapper was a favorite of Bette Davis's and she freely depended on him for his counseling and advice even apart from any movies that they took part in together.

Irving Rapper was born in England, but became an actor and stage director on Broadway while he was a college student at New York University. However, he had always been fascinated with the world of film so when Warner Bros offered him a job as dialogue director in the mid-thirties, Irving Rapper left for Hollywood to begin his career. He had earned his stripes first as a dialogue director and then as an assistant director.

In covering the career of Irving Rapper I am going backwards to the time we worked on the movie called *The Great O'Malley.* In the mid-thirties at Warner Bros., they had many directors of foreign birth who had great difficulty understanding English and their actors. Being of a very patient nature (quite unlike some of the mainstream directors he worked for), he proved indispensible to the greats like Michael Curtiz and William Dieterle. Dieterle happened to be the director of *The Great O'Malley* and because of his and his wife's interest and following to the letter of the science of astrology it caused a bit of a problem on the set. For starters he did not want to direct *The Great O'Malley* because he had no interest in the subject of crime (which was *not* the main theme of this movie), but assumed that it did with Bogie (although he portrayed a family man trying to support his wife and crippled child) and Pat O'Brien as a policeman in the cast. Apparently, he had been promised by Hal Wallis that he would not have to direct certain movies, but by the time he was scheduled for *O'Malley,* Mr. Wallis was in Europe and could not be reached. This left a very unhappy and disgruntled director who had to follow through with his assignment because Jack Warner issued the order that he do so. I'm afraid Mr. Dieterle showed very clearly that he did not like his cast, especially Ann Sheridan whose cheerfulness got on his nerves. In regards to me, he did some nitpicking about a family heirloom of a gold bangle bracelet that I was wearing and that he wanted cut off my wrist. Even Bogie offered that even though I came from poor parents that that bracelet could have come from a dime store. This incensed Mr. Dieterle even more and he ran to a telephone to call Mr. Warner to complain that he had a very uncooperative cast and that he wanted his newest directive about my bracelet obeyed. Mr. Warner was not buying his complaint and told him that the bracelet stayed where it was. From then on Dieterle very rarely spoke to anyone and only mediated through Irving Rapper. Mr. Rapper had the patience of Job throughout the rest of the shooting schedule of the movie and in essence Irving guided us very gently to offset what orders Mr. Dieterle gruffly growled out at us from time to time.

I'll never forget how gentle he was when the problem of the bracelet first came up. I had had that gold bangle on my wrist since I was six months old (gold was continually added year after year with growth) and he could see that my sister and I were quite upset with the order to take it off. During a break Irving brought us a coke and sat us down to discuss the situation. He thought that eventually something would be worked out, but we all needed to give our director time to calm down. It was true that Dieterle had a very volatile personality, but if handled correctly a tantrum would eventually subside and there was no one better than Irving to be a salve for the problems that turned up.

I honestly don't remember seeing Mr. Dieterle at the preview of *The Great O'Malley*, but I do remember Irving Rapper coming over to us after the showing of the movie, congratulating us for a good job well done, shaking Anita's and my uncle's hands and kissing mine. With a pat on my arm he said, "I hope that we work together again sometime in the future." We never did, but he went on to become a successful and a well-appreciated director.

Both Douglas Fairbanks and me being honored at a
show business banquet in Hollywood.

Me and Kirk Douglas (amongst many others) being honored at
The American Cinema Awards.

A Smattering of This 'n That

In life's interesting journey, we meet people who are destined to be life long friends and others who are newly discovered ones. I have never been fortunate to have had a friend starting from babyhood through my adult years (is that an acceptable description for one being a bit long in the tooth?), but that is only because I have been somewhat of a gypsy in my early life by travelling from one country to another. In my particular case I was born in Cape Town, South Africa, but left my country when I was four years old and began my journey from there to England where I appeared on the British stages of The London Palladium and The Royal Albert Hall and even did two movies which, in part, led to my eventual departure for Hollywood to start my career as Warner Bros.' first child star.

During those years in Hollywood I developed deep attachments with my fellow adult actors and actresses, directors and producers, but friendships with kids my own age was difficult because I was pretty well "protected from the outside world" by the cocoon of my studio, home and work. There was no public school for me because if I was not being taught at home by a private tutor, I had a private teacher at my studio. You have read in my other books and now in this one the wonderful experiences that I had with the many icons of the motion picture and music industry. Those experiences probably had a huge mental influence upon me in my growing-up years and I say *mental influence* because in one of life's strange twists I spent the war years from 1941 to the end of 1946 unexpectedly back in South Africa.

However, even though surrounded by family and enjoying the absolutely beautiful country I was born in, I was still carrying America around within my mind and heart.

Probably the closest I came to having childhood friends was when I attended school in South Africa and although that was an uphill climb

Cora Sue Collins and I at Cinecon banquet 2008.

being the newcomer in a group of kids who truly grew up together from the crib, I eventually overcame some of the "stigma" of being a celebrity yet even then never really actually" belonged" to the crowd. The same thing was happening in Hollywood. The child stars that I was acquainted with were also growing up and attending parties together and later on dating "one of their own" and that I had to face once I returned to America. However, it wasn't all gloom and doom. Friendships did develop with renewed social dates with my show-business contemporaries and also to find out, a number of years later, that some of my South African school chums had immigrated to America and made their homes in California. It's a joy nowadays to have bonded very closely with my Capetonian school chum Geraldine and her husband Joe Malamad who have lived in nearby Santa Monica for years. We do socialize and it's fun when they attend many of my public appearances.

After Tony and I had been married for a few years we were ecstatic to find out that I was pregnant. We were living in an apartment in Hollywood at the time, but started to discuss looking for a house we could bring our baby to once it arrived. It was just a matter of a very few weeks when we

Turhan Bey and myself as guest stars.

knew that I was one of those unfortunate women who found it difficult to keep a baby full term when I got the obvious symptom of a miscarriage. Losing that baby was devastating to me; however, my doctor said that we should not give up hope because it was not unusual that after a woman miscarries she soon becomes pregnant again. He was right and I did. Tony and I went ahead with our original plans of finding a small house in a pleasant neighborhood and we were very fortunate in finding just what we wanted in Toluca Lake not a stone's throw away from Warner Bros. studio.

As all young couples do, Tony and I set out to do some furniture shopping and we had them delivered to our new home. I started in organizing the placement of the furniture, our dresser drawers and linen closets and Tony, being the wonderful artist, was kept busy artistically giving the nursery its finishing touches and tending to our back garden and enclosed patio that was going to be great for giving parties.

On one of our visits to my doctor we told him about buying our house and what fun it had been furnishing it; he warned me not to be lifting anything heavy, especially until that crucial three-month period had been reached and even then for me to tread lightly. Having been an active person all of my life, it was hard for me to just sit around for a matter of months, but we wanted this baby so badly that any effort toward having a healthy baby was worth it tenfold. A lot of tension was relieved when Tony and I heaved a big sigh of relief when I passed that three-month crucial period and my baby was still with me.

One morning my telephone rang quite early and it was an operator from Western Union Telegraph Company. In those days when a telegram or cablegram contained bad news the operator warned you about it ahead of time and then asked if you wished to have it read to you. Not knowing what possibly could be bad news, I asked her to please go ahead and read it to me. It had been from Anita telling me that our mother had just passed away in Cape Town and that she would phone me all of the details in another day and for me, in the meantime, to please take it easy. My whole body reverberated in shock as I put down the receiver and just fell apart in a crying spell. Tony was not at home at the time as he was busy working on a script with another man at his house so there was no one to cling to until my emotions had settled down. That took quite a while until I managed to call Tony and tell him the news. He told me that he would be on his way home and it was really a good thing that he did because I started to have bad cramps and the start of what I thought might be another miscarriage.

Sybil Jason BECKY doll.

We rushed to my doctor, who very soon took care of my symptoms and told us, to our relief, that it wasn't a miscarriage, but it could be if I wasn't very careful from here on in. I was told that it wouldn't be necessary for me to be bedridden for the rest of my pregnancy, but I should be walking on eggshells till the baby was born. Eggshells it was and the next call from Anita was a joyous one. She was making plans to come over to help us with the baby a few weeks before it was due and had already booked passage on a ship for that time period. Tony and I both thought who better than Anita to help guide us through the child birth and helping to take care of our baby once it was here. We excitedly got our spare room ready for Anita's visit.

When it came to our baby's arrival, it took place unexpectedly five-and-a-half weeks before she was due. But apart from staying in the hospital to maintain a five-pound weight, Toni Maryanna Drake was a healthy baby, albeit needing to gain some weight which she did after she came to her own home. Toni was named after her father, Tony, and her middle name contained the names of her grandmothers' on both sides: Mary for my mother and Anna for Tony's mother.

Probably one of the happiest periods in my life took place under one roof with Tony, our baby daughter Toni, and my much-loved sister Anita. Anita delighted in describing her newest niece as "my baby's baby" and the beautiful part of it all is that the four of us got along so beautifully and that Tony and Anita acted more like brother and sister than in-laws.

When Toni had gained a sufficient amount of weight, we took my sister to all of the usual tourist attractions like Disneyland and Knottsberry Farm and then later concentrated on nostalgic trips to places Anita knew so well, like Palm Springs and Lake Arrowhead. For the most part, not

Robert Forster and self.

too much had changed from the '40s to 1959 (just a few years later it was another story), so she found it pretty easy to reconnect to places that she knew from our earlier days in California.

It was, without a doubt, a glorious three months that she stayed with us. But with just a visitor's visa and a boyfriend waiting for her in South Africa, she said a tearful goodbye to us and started on her long journey home.

We then prepared to welcome Tony's mother, stepfather Mike, and older sister Ann to our home a mere two days later and, needless to say, it was another wonderful one-month visit. They all spoiled us rotten, as had Anita, and to their delight we repeated our "tourist type" trips that we had done for my sister and we really got a kick out of the bounty of souvenirs that they bought and took back to Pennsylvania with them. After their one month's stay with us was over and we said our goodbyes to them, our little home suddenly seemed so quiet. In a way it was a bit scary for a new mother like me not to have some loving "back-ups" to rely on, but it really was quite amazing how easy it was to get the knack of it and establish a very good daily routine for little Toni and me, which I put into practice almost immediately. Each morning after feeding my little one her breakfast and letting her splash happily in her bath, I dressed her in some comfortable but cute outfits and we were soon prepared for our daily "walks." We took three different routes so that the sights did not get boring either for Toni or myself. The one route was not too far from our house and we usually took it when the weather was a bit overcast and not our usual sunny California weather. This little stopover was just a small but charming coffee shop that was semi-attached to a gasoline station (neither one still there). There was nothing fancy about it, but it was popular with the neighborhood and the gasoline customers for a quick cup of coffee and a cheery greeting from the gentleman who ran the place.

Bob Hope

One day we chose this stopover for our short walk and as we entered the coffee shop we heard Jim (the manager) saying to a gentleman customer, "You see, you are not the only one who is a regular customer." The gentleman turned around and who was it but none other than the great comedian Bob Hope. He made a great fuss over Toni and when he asked me what her name was, he broke out into a grin and said, "I have one at home with the same name only he is a boy."

I never said anything about my show-business background, so we stuck strictly to the subjects of children, family, and Toluca Lake and it was one of the most refreshing conversations I had with a new acquaintance in a long time. He parted with, "Hope to bump into you and your little princess sometime in the future." I smiled to myself at his remark about my little princess referring to my baby, but also unknowingly naming a movie that I had been in when I was a child.

Many years later a longtime friend of mine, "Kid" Chissell, who was an actor and a newspaper columnist, had a bit part on Bob Hope's television show. "Kid" took me along as his guest and I had a great time watching the rehearsals (X-rated) and the taping (G-rated and hilarious) and was amazed how extremely laidback and at ease Bob Hope was whether it was at rehearsals or the taping. If I remember correctly, his guest stars on this particular segment were

George Forman, the world's heavyweight boxing champion, and comedian Don Rickles. Mr. Forman was a very imposing figure, but, surprisingly enough, quite shy, though that may have been because he was not as comfortable appearing as a guest star than he was in the boxing ring. Don Rickles was an entirely different story.

During rehearsals he would leave the set and run around the audience area making obscene but funny remarks and keeping everyone in hysterics. One time he got to the side of my chair and I must have had the look of a deer caught in the headlights of a car because all he did was stare at me with a wicked look on his face which got me to the edge of my seat wondering what would be next. Much to my relief, all he did was wiggle his finger at me and with a huge grin on his face left the audience area and went back to the set.

The rehearsals went along for a while before a break was called and it was then that "Kid" took me up on the set to meet Bob Hope. As soon as my name was mentioned, Bob was quite familiar with my background as an actress and asked if I was intending to continue on with my career. When I told him I was not, he thought it was a shame because he remembered "What a natural little actress you were." He was *very* amused when I told him that this was not our first meeting and mentioned the coffee shop incident. The palm of his hand struck his forehead he said, "I should have known you were in the business. You had all of the signs." After a while I sensed that we were keeping him away from his rehearsal break, so I excused myself and said that it had been a pleasure *formally* meeting him and with a wave of his hand he remarked, "If we keep on meeting this often people are going to talk." Of course, "this often" was once at the coffee shop and many years later at this rehearsal. Who needed writers? He wasn't Bob Hope for nothing!

As I had mentioned previously, everyone in Hollywood knew "Kid" and that was not confined to just people in the industry. His varied acquaintances were fighters (he had been one in the Navy when he was young), politicians, and what the FBI would quaintly call "the boys." In the latter category, my husband and myself were acquainted with one of "Kid's" close friends by the name of Vince Barbi who was also a part-time actor in between doing "other and various type of jobs" for "various other type bosses." We found Vince to be a very sweet man and very protective. That day I found out how protective he was.

When rehearsals were over, and taping was about to begin, "Kid" had to join the rest of the cast on the set. He told Vince to "keep an eye on her." Now, I know what Velcro feels like. Vince never left my side for a second and if anyone approached me he would ask me, "D'ya know dem?" before he would let them get any closer to me, especially the men. My husband and I were amused for years after "Kid" told us that Vince was fond of telling people that he knew Al Capone and that "Capone died in m'ahms." Vince was a character and I doubt seriously if he ever did anyone any harm, but he loved to think that people *thought* that he had.

One morning, back to when Toni was a baby, the weather was a bit overcast so I decided that we would take our shortest walk to the coffee shop. The coffee shop itself was quite small but charming and for the neighborhood and the gasoline customers a handy no-fuss stop for a cup of coffee and a regular cheery greeting from Jim, the man that ran the shop. There were two booths for those who wanted something more than coffee and on this particular day the one booth was occupied by a man reading a newspaper. I asked Jim for a cup of tea and a cookie for Toni to have with her bottle and as we headed for the second booth I happened to drop the cookie on the floor. With a mild expletive I bent down to get rid of the cookie and that brought the newspaper down from the face of the gentleman in the next booth. My jaw dropped and so did the cookie for the second time when I saw that it was none other than...

Oscar winner Westside Story George Chakiris and me.

Donald Crisp

The gentleman that he was, he got up and bent down to get the dropped cookie and said, "I assume that you don't want to ingest this little tidbit." I stammered, "Oh no and thank you, Mr. Crisp," as he deposited it in the wastepaper basket. By this time Jim had come over with another cookie for Toni and said, "I assume you know each other?" Donald Crisp shook his head "No," and I shook my head "Yes," much to the actor's amazement. He then asked, "We do know each other?"

When I started explaining that we had both been in two Warner Bros movies together, *The Great O'Malley* and *Comet Over Broadway,* I got the usual reaction of "Where did those years go? Yesterday you were a little girl and now here you are a married woman and a mother of a baby." I reminded him of the strange fact that although we were in two movies together in neither one did we have one scene together. It was the exact opposite of my relationships with other actors in that I met Donald Crisp more socially than I did at work.

Let me explain. In the thirties there was a large British contingent of actors in Hollywood and they became what one would call a bit clannish in that they attended the same clubs and sporting events together and, of course, entertained at each other's homes. One of the regular meeting places we used to see practically every Brit at were the cricket matches organized and headed by Sir Aubrey Smith. I used to see David Niven and Errol Flynn, Basil Rathbone (a fellow South African by the way) there at most of the cricket matches as well as Donald Crisp. When I was reminiscing about all of those events, Mr. Crisp seemed to really enjoy himself in going back in time. He always consid-

ered me a little girl from Britain, but when I told him I was born in South Africa he said we shared something else in common. For many years everyone believed that he was born in Scotland, but that he was really born in Bow in London, England. However, he did admit to a real love for the Scottish people and even mentioned that one of his favorite movie shorts was a Technicolor one that I starred in at Warners, *Changing of the Guard*.

That afternoon at that little coffee shop went by so quickly and so pleasantly that I was very reluctant to call it a day, but I had to get my little one home for her nap, then to bathe her

Legitimate postage stamps of Antigua and Barbuda Shirley Temple and Sybil Jason.

Book signing with me, Mickey and Jan Rooney 2009.

and wait for her daddy to come home to have dinner and for us to make big fussies and play with her for the rest of the evening. As I departed the coffee shop, this wonderful actor and I both hoped that we would meet again for some more updates, but sadly that was the last time that I saw Mr. Crisp. However, I do thank heavens for film because I can at least still enjoy his wonderful artistry via the television screen.

Book signing of second book *Five Minutes More* 2007.

Book signing of first book *My Fifteen Minutes*, 2005.
Cover features Sybil Jason and Jack Warner.

The second route that Toni and I took was the longest way from our house so we generally landed up there by mid-afternoon. It was a combination of an upscale gift shop, drugstore and one that was equipped with a soda fountain so that I could have a salad for lunch while Toni hungrily busied herself with her midday bottle. All the women behind the counter used to spoil Toni like crazy and it never failed that they would bring her a tiny dish of ice cream for me to feed her and another lady would always gift her with some little toy from the gift shop section. After we got to know everyone by their first names, they gave me the store's private telephone number to call if we weren't going to be in the neighborhood for the next few days. They used to worry if some time had elapsed since our last visit and the possibility that Toni might have been ill. I have to admit that it was a lovely feeling that people felt that warmly toward Toni and me.

Of course, there was always the third route that we took that was pretty close to home yet farther away than the first coffee shop. This needs an explanation because this site was actually on the grounds of Warner Bros. Studio. For all intents and purposes it was a drugstore with a soda fountain and although accessible to the public very few people knew about it except the employees of Warner Bros. and they weren't spreading the news. This drugstore no longer exists because now the whole facility is closed to the public and the rest of the attached buildings have been turned

Book signing. (Godson of cinemaphotographer Jimmy Wong Howe)
Martin Fong and me, 2005.

into offices. There was nothing fancy about the place. It was mainly a
drugstore for the convenience of the Warner employees and a soda fountain for a quick lunch or beverage.

Toni and I were in there often enough to make the acquaintance of a
gentleman who complimented us on our blue eyes. He said my daughter
reminded him of a kid star whose movies he used to edit in the thirties at
the studio. Goose flesh started up my arms when he said that and as calmly
as I could, I asked him if he remembered her name. He smiled and said,
"She was the cutest kid you ever saw and had a beautiful English accent. As
a matter of fact, you can still see her old movies on television nowadays. If
you do, take note of her eyes. They look so similar to you and your
daughter's." I assumed that he didn't remember her name so I asked, "Was
her first name Sybil?" He looked very surprised and pleased and said, "Yes,
it certainly was, but I thought you might be too young to remember her."

I started laughing and the poor man looked a bit puzzled at my reaction
to his comment. As soon as I could get control of myself, I told him, "Please
excuse my rudeness, but I thought your answer was so funny. You see, I *am*

Cinecon banquet, 2008. Me, Betty Garrett & Ann Rutherford.

Taken at a private home celebrity party,
me and Harry Guardino.

Buddy Rogers and I being honored at same banquet as above.

that same Sybil and I do thank you for your compliments." It was the usual reaction with the shake of the head and the disbelief that so many years had gone by that the child he once knew was now a married woman with a baby of her own. After that day we often shared a beverage and talked of "the good old days" and he said that although he still worked for Warners the studio was not quite the same as it used to be. He said that, in part, that was because most of his fellow employees had either retired or died, and he was now one of the few survivors of the thirties on the lot. "A lonely position to be in." I told him that I had similar feelings when my movies were shown on television. Most of the cast and crew of those movies had passed away and if they hadn't they were involuntarily retired, voluntarily retired, or had moved out of the state. He really enjoyed our talks and so did I, but one day as Toni and I headed toward that drugstore a big change had taken place. The area had been closed off and was no longer accessible to the public. By the time my child was older and I started visiting the lot semi-regularly to have lunch or to meet friends in the Green Room (or the Blue Room, as it was then called) through inquiries I found out that my drugstore friend no longer worked at Warner Bros. I remember thinking that I hoped that in his case his retirement was a happy one and perhaps by chance we would meet again somewhere in time.

Finis

I t's been such a pleasure to share my personal memories of the past and the wonderful people who inhabited them to you in book form. Initially, it had not been my intention to write a book. Far from it. My true intention had been to write a letter of complaint to an author whose book I had just finished reading. Even though it is not my habit to go nitpicking about someone else's work, in this case I absolutely needed, both physically and mentally, to let off some steam.

I must explain that for many years it disturbed me that when a well-known personality passes away, how legitimate would his or her biography be handled. Would it be well-researched, would the author try their best to get in touch with the subject's family and friends for data, or would the book be based on apocryphal and salacious tales just so that they could entice the public to buy their books. If it were the latter, did the author consider how the falsehoods would affect the lives of the loved ones left behind or was the main consideration a monetary thing? Looking at this optimistically, I am sure that most biographers do their best and rely on the facts. I will not give the author of the book any more mention or his name because I do not want to carry on the myths that he wrote about a very wonderful woman and actress that I had known very well and had worked with twice in motion pictures. I do not portend to write about people I have never met or worked with, but when I happen to read out-and-out lies about a person who can no longer defend themselves and I happen to know the true facts I do get very upset. In this case the gentleman author picked on two different sites and circumstances where I was there about 90% of the time and knew, without a doubt, that what he wrote was completely false.

I will admit that most people do have some warts in their lives and this lady was no different from anyone else and never hid those facts

MR. & MRS. ANTHONY DRAKE
circa 1958

TONI MARYANNA ROSSI
and her mother Sybil
circa 2006

(*above*) Mr. and Mrs. Anthony Drake circa 1958.
(*below*) Toni Maryanna Rossi with her mother, Sybil.

herself, but the biographer handled it in such a way one could only come to the conclusion that she was morally deficient in many ways and insensitive to other people's time and feelings. It was then I started thinking of all the people I had worked with and although many biographies had been written about them they seemed to be lacking in the personal touch. I wanted the public to get to know them as they were as flesh-and-blood people and the best way I could do that was to write about my personal "back-of-the-scenes" experiences that I had with them. I did that to the best of my ability and I hope that you enjoyed reading it in that way.

I feel that I have led a fortunate life. I had a childhood that I enjoyed immensely. I was able to display my talents without any hardships to battle...I met and married the love of my life for 58 years...we had an incredibly loving daughter, Toni (who so reminds me of my sister Anita who guided me with great love and affection till the day she died). Now I live with Toni, my grandson Daniel, and my son-in-law Phillip and we all get along so beautifully so I deem myself a very lucky woman. If I could change just one thing it would be that 58 years spent with my husband Tony just wasn't enough time. I would have liked 58 more.

LaVergne, TN USA
22 June 2010
187021LV00007B/146/P